The Holodynamic Sta

The Advocate's Manual

Manual I

Books by Victor Vernon Woolf, Ph.D.

Holodynamics: How To Develop and Manage Your Personal Power
The original text

The Dance of Life
Transform your world NOW! Create wellness, resolve conflicts and learn to harmonize your "Being" with Nature.

The Holodynamic State of Being: Manual I
Advocates a course in life that unfolds one's fullest potential for the individual and for the planet.

Presence in a Conscious Universe: Manual II
Detailed training in achieving the state of being present, aligning with one's Full Potential Self, bonding with others, transforming holodynes and unfolding of potential.

Field Shifting: The Holodynamics of Integration: Manual III
Training exercises for integration of field of information from the past, present and future through the relive/prelive processes.

Leadership and Teambuilding: The Holodynamics of Building a New World: Manual IV
The use of a Holodynamic approach within systems as in business and education.

Principle-Driven Transformation: The Holodynamics of The Dance of Life: Manual V
The principles, processes and stories that form the basis for teaching Holodynamics.

The Therapy Manifesto: 95 Treatises on Holodynamic Therapy
An outline of 95 findings from current sciences that apply to the theory and practice of therapy.

The Wellness Manifesto: 95 Treatises on Holodynamic Health
A declaration of findings from current sciences that apply to the health industry.

Elves: The Adventures of Nicholas: The Grid of Agony and The Field of Love
A science fiction story about time-traveling elves who live according to the principles and processes of Holodynamic consciousness and become involved in an intergalactic battle that sweeps a small boy, Nicholas Claus, into shifting the grid of agony into a field of love. How Christmas began.

Intimacy: Develop your Being of Togetherness: How to Create an Open, Dynamic, Effective, Intimate, Living Relationship with Someone You Love

Related Writings

Tracking: The Exploration of the Inner Space by Kirk Rector
The Ten Processes of Holodynamics by Kirk Rector
The above writings can be purchased at www.Holodynamics.com/store.asp

THE HOLODYNAMIC STATE OF BEING

THE ADVOCATE'S MANUAL
Manual I

FOR THOSE WHO ADVOCATE
TAKING THE COURSE OF THEIR FULL POTENTIAL SELF
AND UNFOLDING POTENTIAL FOR THEMSELVES AND
THE PLANET

By
Victor Vernon Woolf, Ph.D.

The processes, concepts and principles
by which a participant in Holodynamics
becomes certified as an Advocate.

The Holodynamic State of Being:

The Advocate's Manual

*For those who advocate taking the course of their Full Potential Self
and unfolding that potential for themselves and the planet.*

Original Illustrations by the author
Cover by Charles Montague
Design by Debbie Drecksel
Others by permission as noted

Library of Congress Cataloging-in-Publication Data

Woolf, Victor Vernon
The Holodynamic State of Being:
The Advocate's Manual
Manual I

ISBN 0-9746431-1-4
1. Consciousness. 2. Science. 3. Psychology.
4. Cosmology. 5. Health. 6. Self Help.
7. Self-Organizing Information Systems.
8. Quantum Theory. 9. Title.

PRINTED IN THE UNITED STATES OF AMERICA

Publisher: The International Academy of Holodynamics
1155 West 4th Street, Suite 214, Reno, NV 89503

Additional copies of this text may be obtained directly through www.holodynamics.com
or from your local distributor.

TABLE OF CONTENTS

THE HOLODYNAMIC STATE OF BEING:
THE ADVOCATE'S MANUAL

INTRODUCTION

This book is the text for the first of a series of courses sponsored by the International Academy of Holodynamics. These courses are called the "Circles of Success" classes and they outline in detail how to be successful in solving complex problems on the planet.

In order to solve some of the problems we are facing, we must become more aware of what is causing the problems and how to create solutions. The main text for this course is *The Dance of Life,* which outlines how complex problems are solved. As the text points out, there is an implicate order to how problems are solved. In the academy, we have outlined a series of courses (the Circles of Success) that reflect this implicate order as it applies to finding solutions to the challenges we are facing. This first manual provides a detailed outline of how to master the first Circle, which is called *the Circle of the Advocate.*

The focus of this writing is on what it means to become an Advocate and how to teach this approach to others. We use a multidimensional approach (Holodynamics) and enter into an embracive state of being. We must *become* the solution. Since we live in a world that is made up of multiple dimensions that are enfolded within what we perceive to be real, and, because we are each individual and unique, we each perceive reality in different ways. It is the perspective of this book that, in order to solve our problems, we must take on a Holodynamic state of being to solve them. In other words, we must become an Advocate. An Advocate is one who advocates solutions.

Chapter One explores what it means to be an Advocate of solutions. Chapter Two deals with how an Advocate is able to empower solutions by becoming *present.* It also deals with how, when you are present, you will naturally begin to teach the whole dynamic to others. Learning how to *find* solutions is part of the solution process and, because the challenges we face today are very complex, the solution process must be *taught.* Solutions cannot be achieved in isolation. So this is also about teaching how to find solutions.

Chapter Three outlines the Circles of Success of the Academy. The first Circle of Success is for Advocates and so the rest of the book is about what every Advocate must know about unfolding potential solutions. Chapter Four outlines the first half of the Unfolding Potential course and Chapter Five outlines the second half. The purpose of this course is to show both the science and the practical skills of how to advocate solutions even when the problems seem irresolvable. In this book, problems are caused by their solutions. As an Advocate, your job is to find the solutions and teach others how to do the same.

CHAPTER ONE

WHAT IS AN ADVOCATE?

HEN PAUL TOWNSEND TALKS ABOUT HOW THERE MORE THAN TEN different dimensions enfolded within our reality, he's telling us that we can expand our view to include more of these dimensions in solving the problems we are facing on the planet. I like his approach and I have tried it and it works – every time! Our limited perception is *causal*. We can't see the solutions because we can't see. We are blind to what is real and thus blind to our solutions. In Townsend's terms, when we see an unsolvable problem, our *P-brane* is too small to handle what is going on. We must open our view to the rest of reality. We must become Holodynamic.

This does not mean that we lack the capacity to solve our problems. No. We have the capacity so allow me to demonstrate how you and everyone you know can become a real Advocate of Holodynamics.

What is an Advocate?

An Advocate focuses on the whole dynamic of the world in which we live and solves problems. Recent discoveries in various fields of science show that we live in a *Holodynamic* reality. An Advocate is anyone who is willing to explore what is real in all dimensions and use that knowledge to create solutions to problems. Those who understand these enfolded dimensions of reality *advocate* Holodynamic reality because it holds the keys to solving even the most complex problems facing the planet.

What does an Advocate actually advocate?

An Advocate advocates Holodynamics. There are many reasons people advocate Holodynamics. Here are a few.

One of the best-kept secrets of modern science is the discovery that everything is made of *information in motion*. Atoms are actually made of *spinners* that contain *frequencies of information* that spin in such a way that they give *form* to matter and actually hold matter in its place. This raises a lot of questions such as: How does matter retain its shape? How do atoms and sub-atomic particles actually remain stable?

According to the best sciences available, matter is able to take shape and we are able to experience life as we do because our world is *multidimensional, holographic, interconnected and dynamic*. Reality is one, whole dynamic information exchange. We are *Holodynamic*. No matter what we were taught in the past, we cannot escape these facts. Anything that disagrees with or denies these facts is an illusion.

In the process of exploring the world of smallness and attempting to understand what matter is made of, scientists have discovered at least 10 *enfolded dimensions* of reality. These enfolded dimensions have been discovered in different sciences: quantum physics, holographics, genomic biology, psychology, mathematics and the science of consciousness, to mention a few. My interest was in applying this new information in situations that were considered "unsolvable problems" of our society. What I found was that every enfolded dimension is essential in order for us to continue to exist. If we leave something out, our chances of survival diminish. So I want to share with you what I found and why I am insisting that you advocate a Holodynamic view of reality.

Not only is matter made of information in motion but, as we have explained more completely in *The Dance of Life,* matter is holographic. Everything is a *projection of information* from more complex dimensions of reality contained within the quantum field of potential. Some of these more complex dimensions of reality are not visible to our holographic senses but they are evidenced in how matter is influenced by quantum states of gravity and other enfolded dimensions of reality. It is estimated that more than 90% of reality cannot be detected by our normal senses. Most of these enfolded dimensions are not visible in our universe but this does not mean they do not exist. There plenty of evidence that they do exist and that we can use the information they contain to solve even our most complex problems.

One such enfolded dimension is referred to as *hyperspace* (Penrose, Hawking, etc.). Hyperspace is the name given to a dimension of reality that is considered to be outside of our space-time continuum. We know it exists because subatomic spinners, electrons and subatomic particles are intimately connected to hyperspace. For example, in physics there are what are called "dualities" that are part of every subatomic particle. Particles are actually made from spinners of information that are being projected holographically from hyperspace. Everything has a *dual* nature that includes a *counterpart in hyperspace* (Hawking).

Another aspect of this is that everything is *conscious*. You can see this in experiments such as those conducted at Temple University in 1984, in which even photons make intelligent choices and can slip into and out of hyperspace at any given opportunity. These remarkable facts have changed our entire view of reality.

The more we learn about this universe, the more we realize that there are many *enfolded* dimensions of reality (Townsend) and, because all of these dimensions are made of information and all of them are conscious, we can use this information to our advantage. As far as we can tell, the world in which we live emerges from a quantum potential field and this quantum potential field gives us our form and holds us in place. According to David Bohm and others, we take form and develop into maturity according to an implicate order. Everything grows according to a pattern.

What makes these discoveries important is that these hidden, enfolded dimensions of reality also contain the *solutions to all of our problems.* The keys to our future are found enfolded within our Holodynamic reality. This is what an Advocate actually advocates: a view of reality that solves our problems and unfolds our potential.

As we become more conscious of our reality, we become more effective in dealing with the challenges of life. We become more capable of understanding the whole dynamic of this conscious universe. We discover that everything is connected and every problem is actually created *by* its potential solution. We are part of one, interconnect, dynamic universe that both creates our challenges and provides everything needed for solutions.

In other words, we live in a Holodynamic world where we are challenged to manifest our personal and collective potential. The key to solving the challenges we face in life is to unfold the natural Holodynamic state of being *present*.

Once we realize that we are each equipped from the beginning to meet every challenge and solve every problem, how then can we possibly do anything else but advocate the solution to the problems we face in our present world?

How do I become an Advocate?

What is required first is that we become aligned with our hyperspacial connection. We must become conscious of who we are, connect with our source (our hyperspacial counterpart or Full Potential Self) and manifest conscious living in a conscious universe. We must become *present*.

This text is written for those who desire to become more present and more effective in solving complex problems on the planet. We can solve our personal problems. We can heal all diseases, overcome all conflicts, balance our biosphere and establish a more sustainable future for humanity and for all of life. We can learn to participate more fully in unfolding our personal and collective potential in this magnificent dance of life.

In order to do this, we must become aware of the different dimensions of reality that are enfolded within the world in which we live. The most primary of all these dimensions is the one that reveals the existence of one's Full Potential Self. Those who make this connection enter *a state of being* wherein all information necessary to solve our problems and meet our challenges is unveiled. This is the doorway to presence.

Those who are aware of the conscious nature of the universe and its enfolded dimensions of reality *advocate* such a state of being and advocate solutions to the challenges we face as individuals and as a planet.

Why do we need to "Advocate" anything?

Most people realize that we live in a time when knowledge is more than doubling every year. The results require immediate intervention for the following reasons:

1. Become conscious of how to manage the rapid advances in technology:

The rapid expansion of technology has spawned a growth that is unparalleled in human history. One of the reasons we need to advocate a Holodynamic view is that people are seeking to accelerate the growth of their own consciousness in order to keep up with the technology. New technology has developed so quickly it has outpaced the development of human consciousness, and taking a Holodynamic view stimulates the development of human consciousness.

As the new information pours in upon us, we find ourselves challenged to meet the demands of our society to learn how to manage things like artificial intelligence, genetic splicing and bionic weapons. We hear about photon transistors that allow quantum computers to run on solar energy and think 2000 times faster than humans. We find ourselves surrounded by bio-robotics and their products. Vast amounts of detailed information floods in upon us every day. If we don't understand the larger picture, it is easy to become lost in the flood of new information.

This is an age of cloning, biodiversity and medical mastery. Even our old, established systems of business and government have become more fluid. Dictatorships dissolve; democracy grows; walls crumble; and money flows toward transparency as new values and ethics emerge among us. It is an age of unbridled hope in the relentless pursuit of perfection. We believe we have conquered nature and are on the way to the stars. These amazing developments are part of an emerging age of consciousness.

2. Handle new telecommunications opportunities:

Our planet has a new *neural* network: the Internet. In an age of satellites and fiber optic cables, the Internet has reached into the depths of separation, across the isolated communities; into the Northern Steps of Russia; into villages deep in the mountains in China; and into the isolated deserts of Arabia and the jungles of Africa. It has crossed the old barriers of religion, politics and culture in every country. This communication system has produced remarkable systems transformations and new global interactions.

3. Utilize new organizational developments:

For organizations, this is an age of unparalleled opportunity. Ancient organizations are dissolving; pyramids of power are transforming; businesses are moving out of central offices and into private homes; and networks of information are bombarding entire populations. Never before has there been such a surge of potentialization. Who among us does not marvel at our accomplishments in radio and television, newspapers, magazines, books, libraries, communication, transportation and mobilization? Who among us does not stand amazed at instant news reporting, video conferencing and international business connections?

4. Transformation of our collective pathologies:

At the same time, this is an age of global self-destruction. Who does not shudder to know that stored within a few miles of our own home may be enough poison gas to kill every living thing on the planet not just once, but more than 100 times! New biologically engineered viruses, neuron bombs, atomic bombs and almost every destructive force possible seem poised now, as part of our possible future, to destroy life on the planet. Pollution has run virtually unchecked for generations until the very foundation of our biological balance is threatened. The entire life of the planet is now in turmoil. The depleting ozone layer, global warming, cataclysmic weather changes and endless wars: the list goes on and on. Humans are collectively immature, self-centered and biologically destructive.

Such information is numbing because the ordinary human being cannot fathom such apparent madness. Furthermore, there seems to be no solution to our collective insanity. We can barely handle the numbing effect of information overload with mass media and the Internet. We struggle with just managing our daily overexposure to personal, social and environmental crisis that confront us daily through the mass media. Emotional and sensational stimulation have exploded into our reality.

The challenge of this "overload" is that we lack, as a people and a culture, the collective common sense to handle it. We have not planned for it, and we have failed, so far, to adopt a state of mind to even comprehend what is happening. We are unable to accept it, let alone manage it and potentialize it. Whether we are willing to accept it or not, *this situation is an invitation.*

What we are facing is the greatest opportunity in the history of humanity and it is time we recognized this reality and stood up and took action. But what action can we possibly take? This is where having a Holodynamic perspective allows us to know exactly what we can do, moment by moment, day by day, year by year.

5. Understand our place on the planet:

For thousands of years we humans were nomads roaming the land and foraging for food. It was only a few thousands of years ago we learned to herd flocks, grow crops and build cities. In the last 300 years, the Industrial Age brought us new machines to do our work. Industry invited people to move from the hardship of the farming life and join the masses needed to operate the factories. Most of the population moved off the farms and into the cities. Now, in the last 50 years, a new age has invited a new type of work.

a. The Age of Information:

This new type of work deals with *information exchange*. The U.S. government reports that more than half of the population of the United States has moved away from the factories and farms and into working on information exchange services. This type of work produces no food or machinery. It produces only information exchange. This is the Age of Information.

b. The declining Age of Abundance:

At the same time, when we step back from our daily demanding schedules and look at the situation we are now facing, it appears as though we are heading for self-destruction. If, for example, the world continues in its present trends, every 20 years the population of the earth will triple. How can we possibly sustain such growth? Even though we have the machines to do our work, new chemicals and new growth stimulants, as well as new fertilizers so we can produce more food, it does not take a rocket scientist to realize we are fast approaching our limits. Our potential to produce food is already so strained that great regions of the planet are locked periodically into cyclic famine. Half the children of the world are hungry almost every day of their lives.

And, if that isn't enough, in the last 40 years we have managed to consume more than half the forests of the planet and we are not replacing the trees! Obviously, this practice is not sustainable. Then we learn that more than 60 percent of the fish have been harvested from the ocean and even from our streams and rivers. Now we are fishing from the hatcheries before the new fish are born! If we continue these practices we will soon ensure our own destruction. We will not have the natural resources to continue with life as we have come to know it. Do you know what to do about this situation?

We are all aware that many species have become extinct in the last 200 years and, with industrial and human pollution, it appears that the entire biological balance of the planet is threatened. We are in the middle of international wars about oil, and, during my lifetime, more than half our oil reserves have been consumed. These reserves cannot be replaced. According to best estimates we have less than 20 years of oil pool reserves left. While we have alternative energy sources, it is now considered by many experts "too late" to implement these alternatives. From this view, a major collapse of our economy and civilization cannot be avoided.

c. Cataclysmic Changes:

If this isn't enough to scare any sane person, we add to these dire predictions the fact that global warming is melting the glacial fields of both the North and South Poles. According to both the Pentagon and the Environmental Protection Agency, these melt-offs have put so much fresh water into the ocean that the Gulf Stream is slowing down. As the Gulf Stream slows, weather patterns become more extreme. Heat from the Equator loses its ability to dissipate evenly, and hurricanes become more frequent and more violent. Winds increase their velocity and, during the hurricanes, the *upper* atmosphere can be *drawn down* causing a *cyclic* effect.

This means the extreme cold of the upper atmosphere may be drawn down to the surface of the earth, causing a series of *cyclic storms* that bring on an almost *immediate ice age*. To add to this alarming news, it is evident that such a thing *has happened before*.

Anthropologists found that about 10,000 years ago, the mammoths of Siberia were *instantly frozen solid*. They still had food in their mouths. The only tenable explanation is that the upper atmosphere was drawn down onto the surface of the earth into cyclic storms that froze everything and caused the last Ice Age.

We know from satellite pictures that the Gulf Stream is already slowing. We also know that the ice fields of the Antarctic are collapsing into the ocean. These ice fields and the melting poles have caused the ocean level to rise one inch in the last three years. If the Ross Shelf in the Antarctic collapses, the ocean level will rise an estimated *18 feet*. According to the satellite pictures, *the Ross Shelf is already cracking*. More than 1,200 of the world's leading scientists have signed a petition stating that this is now considered *the most critical event in the history of humanity*. Add to this the latest reports on the methane gas being emitted from the Eastern Siberia tundra as it melts. thus releasing more carbon dioxide into the air and more than doubling the global warming effect. Global warming seems irreversible.

d. The Good News!

Those who are informed realize that we are *losing it* as a planet. So demanding has been our growth that the human race has been referred to as *a virus* that is *killing* the planet. Still, in light of all this, this is good news. Yes. It is *good* news.

*It is good news because every problem is an invitation to find solutions. Every problem is created **by** its solution. How do we know? We know not only because the new sciences show us that every set of circumstances is driven by potential, but, in addition, we know that we live in a conscious universe and that we are each born under a covenant to meet these challenges. Furthermore, we each have a counterpart in hyperspace that is willing to help. The dynamic growth of technology, our overpopulation, consumption, pollution, global warming and our potential for self-destruction are an invitation to apply our discoveries and our multidimensional reality to solve our problems and manifest their potential solutions. And this is what Advocates do.*

What can I do?

More and more people are asking: "Is there anything I can do that will make a difference? How can we turn the tide on these self-destructive trends?" The answer is "Yes! You can become a Holodynamic Advocate!"

Most people are not aware of what can be done. Each day we get entwined in meeting our daily needs. Caught on the grid of survival, we find it difficult to lift ourselves above our immediate need for clothing, shelter and food. We must, after all, pay the rent. It's not much different among the affluent, for whom the distractions are different but the results are the same. Many people with great resources are impotent because of their personal and collective self-interest and self-indulgences.

One of the challenges we face is that we are locked into a collective consciousness that keeps us busy on our path. Listening to the daily news shows crisis after crisis as news reporters seem to go into feeding frenzies for anything that will draw our attention. As you know, what draws the public attention turns out to be mostly negative news. It's crisis after crisis. With the negative news come very few solutions. Torn apart by crisis after crisis, there is little hope in the public mind for solutions, so we just go on cruise control and do our jobs. There is very little good news - and this is also good news.

This is an age of unparalleled potential destruction and it is also an age when we face a corresponding potential of unfolding unparalleled solutions. The new developments, the new information, the new sciences, the new discoveries and the new understanding of reality provide every tool we need to manifest solutions to every problem we have created. Every one of our problems and challenges are opportunities.

The light and the dark, the good and the bad, the rich and poor are part of the dance of life and, once we understand the dance, we can advocate solutions. We can advocate *life* in the face of *death*, *creativity* in the face of *destruction* and *presence* in the face of *division*. We can remember what we have forgotten. We can remember the whole dynamic. This is what you can advocate.

Why should anyone advocate what you say?

This is not about advocating what any individual says. This is about the whole dynamic. It is about the Holodynamics of life. It is beyond the need for a belief, a school of thought or a path to follow. It is an acknowledgement of what *is*: what exists in reality. It is based upon *what works* and *what is known* in the old and new, the cultures and the sciences; it is an integration of what works and what gets results in this Age of Information. This is an inclusive, encompassing multidimensional look at what is real and how to solve complex problems.

Are there any books about this?

This text accompanies the book *The Dance of Life* and is the first of a series of texts that contain tested, working principles, processes and exercises that help people accelerate their own consciousness. These books go along with a greater body of support literature (see References) and each adds to a wider understanding of the conscious nature of reality and how we can each become part of the solutions to the challenges we face and teach this information to others.

What this text is saying is that once a person *gets* the nature of reality, it is natural to *advocate* a way of life that includes all the information and the whole dynamic of life. To leave anything out, to separate one's thoughts, feelings or actions from the whole dynamic, is to *forget* and thus to enter into a series of *games* that eventually will lead to self-destruction.

Why leave anything out? Why not advocate that all information is valuable as part of what makes life work? Why not advocate Holodynamics? It works. It gets better results. It includes everything and so you have nothing to lose. It is natural. It is a state of being in harmony with nature and the universe. All we have to do is *re-member* our nature and become once again connected to the Holodynamic reality of Nature.

Who are Advocates?

Advocates of Holodynamics come in all shapes and sizes, all colors, cultures, beliefs, religions, species and races. Holodynamists can be found in every country. They are people who remember that we are all part of the same team on this satellite called Earth. Everything and everyone is part of one dynamic, living information field.

They know that everything is made of information in motion. The universe is dynamic. It is consciousness. Every photon, subatomic particle, molecule, cell, animal, plant, person, planet and solar system, is part of a living, dynamic, intelligent system. This immense information system is not limited to the boundaries of the speed of light or the dimensions of space and time. It is hyperspacial and multidimensional. It is cross-cultural; embraces all beliefs; and spans the entire history of humanity, here and elsewhere.

Understanding this allows us to draw upon the deeper dimensions of reality in order to handle what is happening here and now. It allows us to experience life in all its magnificence and grasp the cup of potential, dip it into the potential field, and drink it up more fully.

What happens to me when I become an Advocate?

Once you advocate a Holodynamic view of reality you will soon find yourself more able to solve those "very complex" problems: those that seem "unsolvable" to others. You will learn to experience more consistently that *state of being* wherein your internal world aligns and harmonizes within itself. This personal state of being prepares you to align with the potential of the entire planet. You align your *being* with Nature.

You will find yourself walking with people like Kirk Rector, who left his beautiful home in Hawaii, traveled to Russia in the late 1980's, and amidst the hardest of circumstances, began to share the Holodynamic information with people throughout the (now former) Soviet Union.

Thanks to people like Kirk, there are thousands and thousands of people who have discovered the whole dynamic and learned how to potentialize. Many of these people are now helping to potentialize their entire country and some are working together to spread the potentializing processes to other countries. Once you *get* the whole dynamic, it is impossible to take away your choice, diminish your personal power, or create the illusion of dependency. You become *present*, part of the solution and capable of creating extra-ordinary results.

What does it mean to be "Present"?

To be present means to tap into all those dimensions of one's hyperspacial Full Potential Self so the *real you* can be consciously present in your body. This writing is about a course in becoming *present*; that is, aligning with the source of your information field. It's a specific state of being. It's a harmonic. It's taking the course of your fullest potential. I call this the state of being *present*.

Presence gives you access to the dimension where *your menu of options is created*. Presence creates such dynamic changes that just alignment can mean overcoming diseases that are often highly resistant to being cured by any other means. It can mean living with such passion that you could never have imagined life without this connection. Presence unveils *your life plan*. It allows you to live outside and inside time at the same time.

It also means having great impact upon others. It is almost impossible, once you have mastered presence, to live anything less than totally. You advocate living life to its greatest potential and you naturally teach others about how to accomplish the same thing. Advocates of such a view pledge everything they have to taking a course in life that reflects their fullest potential. You become aligned with life, an intimate part of the whole dynamic.

You realize that how you define yourself cannot be confined to just the unique individual you are, separated from the whole. You are unique. I am too. But you and I are part of the whole dynamic of life. We are *individuals and the collective both at the same time* and also *outside of time*. Understanding this part of reality opens the door to solutions to everything we are facing.

How can we find solutions to problems?

The central focus of this course is to find solutions to everything we are facing. Each of us has spent most of our lives preparing for *this* moment in time. What makes a Holodynamic approach more effective in this moment in time is that we are able to unfold life potential in *all dimensions of time* in this moment of time.

As our awareness grows, we align with information fields that control personal and collective consciousness among all life forms and among humans and nations in all dimensions of time. We become aware of how to shift these fields from parallel worlds, and from the past. We can even integrate the future into the present. We **become** *the future and advocate the solution that we actually found.*

How do I become an Advocate?

You <u>choose</u> to become an Advocate. No one is going to look over your shoulder and inspect how well you are doing. No one will require that you know some body of information or pay a fee or join an organization. *Your choice* is all it takes. Well, it also takes focus and dedication to reach into the information fields and shift them. Learning emerges from deep within the quantum field of potential. It is not just a matter of rational understanding of the facts or of emotional empowerment. It is choosing an all-inclusive, personal state of being present. Who would want anything less for themselves and for the planet?

Advocates choose to take the course in life that aligns with their Full Potential Self. In this state of be-

ing, you have given yourself permission to actually experience everything you will be advocating, to go through the transformations personally and collectively and solve the problems we are facing on this planet.

Are there any steps involved in becoming an Advocate?

There are natural steps involved. As your potential emerges, you, like everyone else, will be going through different stages of development. These are outlined in the Circles of Success program of the Academy. When it comes right down to it, these are natural stages and you, like everyone else, have half a dozen stages of development. Here are examples.

The most basic one, the one that emerges first, is the **physical** manifestation of your body. You already have passed through this stage. You realize that everyone must have *form* in order *to manifest potential.*

What adds to the interest is that your body is composed of symbiotic life forms that are millions of years old. These life forms are held in *coherence* by the action of multiple dimensions of reality (quantum, holographic, etc.) that work together to create the biological field of your body. Your body is an extremely complex information field made up of billions of life forms.

From the complexities of your physical body emerges your **personality**. Your personality is an even more complex information field. You bring with you an arsenal of personal characteristics that make up the matrix of your own consciousness. You also develop new characteristics as part of the unfolding of your own personal potential. Your personality is unique, complex and multidimensional.

From out of the matrix of your personality emerges a consciousness of **relationships**. Relationships are even more complex. Relationships are developed among individuals but they also are inherited, culturally created, personally developed and are part of a multidimensional field of holographic information systems (holodynes). We manifest *a being of togetherness* with each other. Each relationship includes a beyond-time connection. We are hyperspacial beings and we are manifesting covenants we made outside of time. This is another step toward becoming an Advocate.

People also organize into **systems**, each with complex interactions of multiple dimensions. Our systems grow through natural stages of development as the collective consciousness of the entire community emerges. Different cultures, societies, religions, corporations, governments and social systems each go through stage of their own development. Things get more and more complex as your consciousness emerges into the systems to which you are connected. The information builds upon itself as it expands.

These dynamics are driven by enfolded, living **principles**. Love, faith, integrity, honesty, and a host of principle-driven dynamics are manifest. These principles have developed their own causal potency and weave a multidimensional influence within entire fields of information from the past, present and future. They are part of the infrastructure that holds reality together.

Finally, you emerge as an individual who is part of the **universal** state of being. At this stage of development you realize your connectedness to everything, everywhen and everywhere. You are able to access the multiple complexities of reality, share information and create conscious change. You are able to dance the dance of life fully, participating in the dynamics in harmony with life.

We call this natural, self-organizing, emergence of your self *the stages of development*. Each stage reflects an *implicate order of consciousness*. You will be experiencing all six as you take the course of your Full Potential Self. Your friends, family members and associates will experience your shift in consciousness.

Your alignment cannot help but impact them as well. All information is connected. Once you become conscious of Holodynamics, whether you know it or not, you will become an Advocate.

Why should I be an Advocate?

In general, why not advocate all levels of potentialization? Why not maintain a good physical and personal growth program, one that develops effective relationships, gives you the ability to team up with others and become more principled and universal in your perspective? In a way, this book is about establishing a *conditioning* program in which you learn to keep in good health, to nurture your body, exercise, and become an example of good habits. You do the same in handling your personality and your relationships.

You will be advocating a state of being at your fullest potential in every way so that nothing blocks your potential. When you do this, others actually *catch* your state of being. It is the same in principle at every level of the built-in order of your information fields. Information spreads. It's been spreading ever since life first formed on the planet.

What results can I expect?

Even a quantum computer can *reset itself* by *changing one byte*. Once you choose to take the course of your Full Potential Self, you choose to take charge of your inner world, accessing and transforming your own personal information fields. Once on this path, **the collective resets itself**. It is an amazingly simple transformation process of potentializing.

I wrote this book so you could have access to specific information and processes that give you tools for potentializing. This also means potentializing your personal holodynes.

Holodynes are self-organizing information systems that have developed the power to cause things to happen. Some holodynes are still immature and thus are not working to our best interest. Some are even self-destructive to us. These holodynes must be transformed if we are to survive. Transforming holodynes means helping them change into new, more effective, mature holodynes. It means integrating them into new patterns. This means developing chosen, new, mature concepts and processes and transforming the immature holodynes into their fullest possible potential. Once transformed, they can integrate with coherence into your personality. It means applying this new information into your everyday life.

As an Advocate, you demonstrate not just an understanding of Holodynamic principles, but a willingness to stretch and grow as you *take the course of your Full Potential Self.* It is a commitment to relate openly, honestly and responsively to reality, to team up with others, and to *hold the field* as you potentialize together. In this way, you *advocate* a way of life in harmony with people and supportive of Nature. Once you take the course of your Full Potential Self, you realize that all life is a Holodynamic community, and you walk with *presence* among your friends, family and associates, and you bond with Nature.

What is this book about?

I would like to welcome you to a principled view of reality wherein community life holds a collective field for potentializing your life and life on the planet. This book is about taking the course of your Full Potential Self. This is *our* course, *together.* This is a course about *you* but it is also about *us.* It is a course about reaching into your potential and manifesting it *by choice.* It is also a course about *community* and *life* and *potentializing the planet.* It's about success and love and designing your (our) destiny. It's for potentializers who choose to advocate a style of life that works *now* and *prepares us for a better future.*

This is not the only book involved in this quest. In this book we will discuss various stages of development as you increase in personal power. There is additional training for those who want to consult with others (Consultants). There is also continued training for those who want to help facilitate deeper inner growth and social change (Facilitators). There will be training for those who want to teach as teams (Presenters) or on their own (Teachers) and for those who want to master more complex aspects of living a Holodynamic lifestyle, creating projects and help others do the same (Master Teachers). We will be discussing this in more detail later in this text.

There are also additional courses on special subjects. *Intimacy,* for example, is a special course as is *Freedom from Addiction,* the *Holodynamics of Business, Abundance* and *Wellness.* There can be courses for anyone who wants to help others learn to apply the advanced concepts enfolded within the study of Holodynamics so we have organized The International Academy of Holodynamics that officially offers these courses. In some countries there are local academies that are operating as part of the international program.

Each course offers a specific body of information. Each has its own text. This is the first text in a series that prepares you to advocate Holodynamics. These texts contain the heart of the information around which the Holodynamic seminars are taught and they contain the key processes by which you can master the principles and processes that unfold consciousness and solve complex problems. These books also demonstrate how to teach these principles and processes to others. It will help guide you through the processes of certification in the International Academy of Holodynamics.

You've already gone through part of the course just getting here. Congratulations! Through our joint commitment, we will help you create a vortex of energy and information that will potentially empower you for the rest of your life, and, through our continued community, we can shift the field around the world. We can *reset* our biological balance and transform our immature collective.

Who are some of the Advocates?

I am an Advocate and I look forward to a long enriching relationship with you. I honor you for your state of being; for the love you *are* and the power you bring; for your mind and will; for what is to come; and for that which we have already begun. This work is designed to help you move through the natural stages of emergence so you can better manifest who you are in reality. I trust you will co-create with us an ever-improving set of tools for those who choose to take this course.

When Natalia Maslova was exposed to Holodynamics, she went to work and designed a special book on how to teach English to Russian students using holodynes. Not only is she head of the Education Department of the Academy of Natural Science in Russia, but she is now recognized for her remarkable book on teaching Russian students the English language. She now teaches teachers to use Holodynamic potentializing processes.

Someday, on the streets of Salt Lake City, Utah, you may meet Pat Barry, who left a cryptic message on my phone awhile ago. We had run out of books on Holodynamics because of my long absence in Russia. I had not heard from Pat since her husband had died of AIDS years ago. "Vern," she said, "Get me some more books. I am keeping 35 AIDS patients alive by using your book *Holodynamics*. We have run out of books. Please, get me more books." We got her more books.

There is an almost invisible community of people who understand the Holodynamics of reality. Among them are the quiet majority who are dedicated to advocating a way of life that takes the course of their Fullest Potential. They are equally dedicated to assisting others in doing the same. These are some of the Advocates of Holodynamics.

So it is with love, appreciation, and as your eternal friend, that I write this series. I hold a field for you and for us, that we may master the Holodynamics of life.

Chapter Two

You Keep What You Give Away

THERE IS AN ANCIENT ADAGE THAT SAYS: "YOU KEEP WHAT YOU GIVE AWAY." I seldom have seen this adage at work better than in the life of one of my high school teachers.

I can remember only few really good teachers in my life. One was Mr. Levy, my 11th grade psychology teacher at Stathscona High in Edmonton, Alberta, Canada. He used to raze us mercilessly. He was always talking about things in our personal lives and joking about our relationships. He knew his subject matter and he knew his students and above it all, there was something charismatic, almost magical, about him.

He was a teacher. He knew it, we knew it. It was more than his understanding of the subject matter and it was more than his understanding of his students. It was his *state of being.* He did not put on the cloak of being a teacher when he came to school. He *was* a teacher. Yet he never once (that I can think of) actually *taught* anything.

The best words I can find to explain what happened when we were in his class were the words that he "facilitated learning." He was full of discovery. He engaged us all in the excitement of living a life in which we could explore new views, discover new things and apply ourselves in new ways to every situation of life. Life, for Mr. Levy, was a dynamic process of continual discovery.

Experiencing Mr. Levy brought out in me a dimension of myself I did not know existed. He set an example (what I have come to call a *field*) into which I *emerged.* I *caught* his natural enthusiasm. I realized the world needed more teachers like Mr. Levy and, as I see it now, his example inspired in me the latent teacher I was to become. I became a teacher or, more precisely, the teacher in me *emerged.* My potential unfolded. I began my career as a science teacher. I will never forget the excitement of being with the students every day, experimenting in science and learning to explore life.

At the same time, I was invited to teach an early morning religion class for high school students and, at 6:30 each morning, a small group of students and I would explore life from a religious point of view. When Dale Tingey, the head of the Church of Jesus Christ of Latter Day Saints Department of Education, came to visit my class one morning, he came up to me after and said, "You are the best teacher I have ever seen. Will you come and work with us in the church?"

I had a wife and family of three children at the time, and, after we discussed it, we moved to Salt Lake City where I began to teach religion to high school students. It did not matter what the subject was to me. What mattered was *the presence of the teacher in the life of the students.* I moved on to teach religion in college and university. I took my master's degree in religious education and eventually began to teach other teachers.

Assignment 1: Gather together with some friends or in a study group (a Holon) and begin with a discussion of what makes a good teacher. Make a list. Keep a record.

The issues surrounding religion awoke in me a desire to learn more about how faith, morality and ethics function in the lives of my students. My focus began to expand from theology into the deeper dimensions of how people thought, and how moral and ethical behavior emerged within their consciousness. This inquiry led me into world religions, the integration of science and religion, and eventually into the anthropology of human thought.

In order to better understand how consciousness develops, I received my Ph.D. in developmental psychology. My passion for exploring consciousness led to several breakthrough discoveries in consciousness. This is where *tracking, reliving, preliving* and most of the processes taught in the course on Holodynamics were first developed and tested. I applied quantum physics, for example, to developmental psychology and what emerged was a new model of the mind. I began to apply the findings to problems facing my community.

Assignment 2: Discuss in your Holon: Does consciousness actually "grow?" Write your thoughts. Keep a record. Be prepared to speak for two minutes on this subject without notes and without notice.

During the original stages of discovery, before Holodynamics was founded as a formal educational approach, I was working with drug abusers in Provo, Utah, in the late 1960s. By this time in my life, I was fairly well trained in the linear models of education and psychotherapy. I was also trained in the spiritual emotive dynamics of the Christian church, but I was amazed to find out that real solutions existed in a dimension beyond anything I had ever been taught. It was the exploration of this more expansive, inclusive view (that I eventually called *Holodynamics*) that led to such phenomenal successes in what came next.

As Director of the Mental Health Association for Utah County, it had come to my attention that more than 50 percent of the high school students in Provo and Orem were "on drugs." It may have been my expanded awareness of things but, quite naturally, I wanted to find out if, by using a more Holodynamic approach, we might help to solve the problems involved when young people take drugs. With some very interesting interventions, I was drawn into the problems and solving drug abuse in my local community became "a project".

Within a few months we had written a federal grant, organized a county drug rehabilitation program and established six drug rehabilitation centers (The Gathering Places). In less than two years, the Gathering Places provided the driving force behind the basic elimination of illegal drug use in six cities in Utah County. These results were so impressive I launched into a lifetime of exploring the solutions to complex problems. The more I focused my attention on a specific problem, the more I became convinced that everything *is* made of information and complex problems can be solved through restructuring that information.

I worked my way out of a job doing drug rehabilitation, and my next program was to open a private family therapy clinic and focus on the high percentage population of mentally ill in my community. Working with families of those who had *identified patients* (Satir) in the mental hospital, I began to teach family members the principles of Holodynamics.

These principles were distilled into 10 processes and, as it turned out, these processes were the key ingredients that helped each family transform their own mental patterns and then teach their *identified patient family members* to do the same. Over eighty percent of the Utah Valley Mental Hospital's patient loads, including many schizophrenic patients, were able to leave the hospital under the care of their families and make a positive contribution to their community.

So successful was the Holodynamic program that other people began to focus on special problems they wanted to solve. Taking a Holodynamic view was central to a prison reform program at the Point of the Mountain prison in Utah. People, who had family members or friends in prison, visited them and taught them Holodynamic principles. They *tracked* them, helped them *relive* their past and *prelive* their futures. Many prisoners, even hard-core offenders, were able to transform their lives.

Assignment 3: Discuss what this statement means: "You keep what you give away!" Create three stories that demonstrate this principle.

The statement: "You keep what you give away!" was how, for example, Brad, a young man who spent two days and nights beating his beautiful young wife to death, came to find himself again. Confined to the hell of maximum security and condemned by everyone in his society, Brad was approached by his sister-in-law Launa, and mother-in-law Brenda, who had learned about Holodynamics.

When I first met Launa and Brenda, they were so filled with hate for Brad that, when they "took the course" and realized *their hate was about learning to love unconditionally*, they became Holodynamists. Their entire lives changed.

They visited Brad in prison and began to share information with him. He caught the message of their new state of being and was able to transform his holodynes in the process. He began to teach others in the prison and soon the work began to spread to other prisons. Brad kept what he gave away.

Likewise, the juvenile courts in Ogden, Utah, and in Las Vegas, Nevada, were impacted to the degree that youth offenders were teaching one another to transform their lives. This effort provided hundreds of young people with new, productive lifestyles.

Jason, for example, was 14 years old and a physically small, wiry, brilliant, rebellious, uncontrollable teenager. He was labeled by the system as "sociopath-schizophrenic." The supervisor of the juvenile detention facility explained to me that Jason "had no hope for a future". At my suggestion, the supervisor ordered Jason to attend the Holodynamic class.

Within minutes Jason took charge of the entire group. It took an hour and a half, with Jason in the center of a room filled with 190 counselors and another 150 young people, before he finally *got* the Holodynamic message. Sixty days later I went to the graduation of those 150 young people. When a tall, well built young man was reporting on his plans for the future, suddenly Jason jumped up and challenged him. "You are conning us!" he declared.

Then I watched as Jason became an Advocate. He fearlessly faced a man, twice his size, and took him through the process of finding his full Potential Self. He *got* it and his friend *got* it. He turned to me and said, "Dr. Woolf, I learned more from this course than I did from the course of my whole life." His transformation was contagious. The entire group was alive with the possibilities. Jason kept what he gave away.

Week after week I was involved in teaching, testing and teaching some more. My path took me into testing the Holodynamic approach in solving complex problems in large corporations. I taught business courses in such organizations as Bank of America, Boeing Aircraft and Toyota of America. Many of the trainers in these organizations got the message and began to teach Holodynamics. It took various forms, and some of those companies are still teaching Holodynamics. Good information spreads fast and is endearing and enduring.

I began to focus in on what I considered to be the top priority problems of collective consciousness in the world. I was particularly concerned about the Cold War. We were spending trillions of dollars on this battle between the giant nations of the world. In United States our annual defense budget was set at more than $350 billion per year. Why were such large sums of money being spent on a military situation when there were so many other uses to which the money and resources could be directed?

No sooner had I begun to focus on the Cold War than I was invited by Brenda Marx Hubbard and Ramah Vernon to visit Russia to serve as part of the Peace Commission in the Soviet-American Dialogues for Peace. I was thrust into intense negotiations. The heat was on and taking a Holodynamic approach was of great value in dealing with the challenges.

By the late 1980s, when the Cold War between Russia and United States was beginning to thaw, I became part of *the 10 Americans for the success of Peristroika* and used Holodynamics to help with the turnaround of the former Soviet Union from Communism to a free enterprise society. Holodynamics proved to be so successful in Russia and the Republics that training programs were established in more than 100 cities. Hundreds of teachers were certified to teach Holodynamics.

During those years of the early '90s, I also turned to the *hot* war in the Middle East between Arab nations and Israeli Zionists. Ramah Vernon had seen what we were able to accomplish in Russia and turned her focus on the Middle East. I got there the second week into the program and was thrust into direct contact with the Palestinians. The results were so extraordinary that I was led into broader and broader aspects of unfolding the potential of education and communication networks around the planet. These accomplishments are written about in detail in *The Dance of Life*. In my own life, I kept what I gave away.

Assignment 4: Create a two minute speech on what you consider to be the most pressing issues facing humankind at this time. Discuss your view in your Holon. Write notes, keep a journal and be prepared to present your view without prior notice.

ADVOCATES IN ACTION

Advocates began to write about their experiences using Holodynamics. For example, Kirk Rector wrote two books (*The Ten Processes of Holodynamics* and *Tracking*); David and Svieta Provalska wrote the book *Holodynamic Living* (in Russian); and Natalia Maslova did a masterful job on *How to Teach English*.

Luba Hocklova, a psychologist who lives in Moscow, Russia, has used Holodynamics in her therapy clinic and has been instrumental in teaching thousands of people the processes of self-potentialization. In order to further assist her in her work, I wrote *The Wellness Manifesto: 95 Treatises on Holodynamic Health* (see References). This book takes the findings of science and applies this new information to the field of health, including mental health; and to the field of psychotherapy. Luba and a group of more than 100 (mostly Russian) psychologists have been so successful in their approach that they are now seeking to establish Holodynamic Psychology as an official branch of psychology throughout the world.

These people who advocate a Holodynamic view and teach the processes by which consciousness emerges each have a story to tell. Each has developed a life that produces extraordinary results. Tatiana Shepel is from Habarovsk in the Far East of Russia (which is about the size of Canada). There are seven major cities in her region and Tatiana has helped develop Holodynamic centers in four of those cities and has active programs in the other three.

Tatiana's first contact with a Holodynamic view came from Olga Provalska, a young Russian woman who, as an Advocate, knocked on the door of the mental hospital where Tatiana worked as a psychiatric nurse. The mental hospital was like a small motel with rows of rooms connected by a hallway. The rooms had little more than a mattress for patients.

Tatiana had to admit that the staff was more than frustrated because their influence upon patients produced so little the way of positive results. She could not afford to attend a seminar in some faraway city so she suggested that Olga invite me to come and teach her and her associates. Khabarovk has been described as "in the middle of nowhere" because there are miles and miles of the Far East wilderness on all sides of the city. I decided it might be an interesting region to teach Holodynamics. Looking back on it now, I realize that neither Tatiana nor I had much of an idea of what would happen. Tatiana *got* Holodynamics.

She became so intent on processing patients that the administration of the mental hospital became alarmed. She was emptying out their mental facility! Born and raised as they were under the confinements of Communism, she soon found it was more effective to quite her job and open her own Holodynamic Center. She inspired others and soon she had groups from other cities seeking training and wanting programs in their own communities. She began teaching not only the courses on Holodynamics, but she applied the principles to aid in the restructuring of the social and economic structure of the Far East. Her program "Noosphere Education" sponsors Holodynamic training in everything from tourism and ecological balance to self-esteem classes.

Those who advocate a Holodynamic view assert that every person has the right to good information and quality education. People have not only the right to good information, but they also have the right to learn how to manage and apply the information. Tatiana Shepel, Kirk Rector, Luba Hocklova and many thousands of others have been making this information available to an ever-expanding number of people who have traditionally been isolated from information for centuries.

Education is an ongoing process by which people expand their consciousness. It is an ever-expanding sense of presence and presence is the key to life. For me, this is one of those *universal* truths. Every religion is dedicated to this aim. Every therapist, school system and training program holds a similar goal. It is encouraging to know that there are certain things that can be done to accelerate our expansion into presence.

What is being taught?

In the International Academy of Holodynamics we teach *10 processes* that show how to develop presence. We will teach and practice these basic processes as part of this educational program in this series of manuals.

Any educational tools - not only the ten processes taught in these courses, but other tools, such as computer-assisted programs, personal transceivers, mentoring and work programs - can aid people. We provide *tools* for everyone's *toolbox*, so to speak. Every educator needs a tool box.

These tools set a new foundation for understanding each person's nature as conscious beings. Each person is part of an ongoing quest that prepares participants to take their place in building a better future. In a world where only 17 percent of the people have access to a phone, where old information perpetuates continued pathology at a rate that now threatens the life of the planet, it becomes our moral and ethical responsibility to do everything we can to transform this situation.

This is why I am telling you this story. I am one person. I believe that *if anyone can, I can.* I also believe that *if I can, you can. We can.* Each of us can do more. We can do everything needed to potentialize the planet. It is a matter of choice.

Assignment 5: Pick a companion and discuss what you, as a person, can do to make a difference in the world? Write down your observations in your personal journal. If you do not have a personal journal, get one. You will need it in the future.

Create a brief presentation on what you can do to make a difference in the world.

Together we can make a difference in consciousness. Who knows what impact a single idea might have upon the life of others? Who knows what actions will lift our world to the heights it needs to unfold our magnificent potential together? This is why I accepted the invitation to be involved in telecommunications and information services.

It is why I became the Director of The International Academy of Holodynamics and formed alliances with schools and universities around the world. It is why I put so much time and energy into developing personal transceivers and education programs. These are start-up programs but they are a beginning of a new approach to life and a new wave of consciousness.

We can improve the quality of education and thus improve the quality of life for everyone. It is a movement that cannot be stopped. No one is in charge. It is happening and it will keep on happening. It is part of the *geni-in-us*. It is why I have always made myself available to teach, track and apply the Holodynamic processes in my own life and among my friends and associates.

This is *Holodynamics* in action. It is walking the talk, aligning with life and surfing the wave of our emerging potential. It is the consciousness of *presence*.

WHAT CAN I DO?

As people become more aware of what we are facing in life, the desire to make a difference in creating a sustainable future is swelling like a rising tide. Here are some of the things people have found that they can do that makes a real contribution to the future.

You can open the door.

Holodynamics includes all dimensions of reality and the integration of every school of thought. It includes information regarding parallel worlds and the application of all information to the solving of problems and the unfolding of potential in every set of circumstances. What stops you from learning about everything on the planet? Nothing! All you have to do is open the door.

You can take the course:

Those who teach (really teach) have integrated the whole dynamic of life into their own personal state of being. Perhaps it would be more accurate to say that they have focused their state of being in such a way that people around them are inspired to learn, to discover and unfold more and more of their own potential. So it is not so much a technique or a body of knowledge. It is more of a *state of being* in which one *takes the course*. You *commit to follow the course of your own Full Potential Self.*

You can be internally referenced:

You can tell when people are "in" their fullest potential because they are *internally referenced*. They require little, if any, external motivation. They are, by their very state of being, advocates. They are *inclusive* in their love and devotion to reality and are *naturally drawn* to possible applications that improve the quality of life of people and the planet. When you reach into your natural state of being, you know you are part of one whole dynamic reality.

You can expand your *P-brane*:

A Holodynamic view of reality includes every dynamic, so those who advocate this view are interested in every dynamic of life. This includes every branch of knowledge, every species and culture, every belief system of human beings and every phenomenon of nature.

This does not mean you have to know every mathematical proof of every physics formula. Rather it's about each person developing a Holodynamic view of reality and life as one-whole-dynamic system of self-organizing information.

Nor is this is a mechanistic view. There is no *absolute* truth out there waiting to be discovered. Rather, it is the recognition of the universe as a living, dynamic interactive information system, responding to each of us and changing from moment to moment.

You can take it personally:

Reality is viewed as an intimate involvement with every aspect of the universe. It reflects itself in how you think and act. The result of this state of being is that your actions make a difference in life. Reality is responsive. Life is dynamic. Consciousness is universal.

You can solve problems:

Problems are no longer "problems" but are *solutions waiting to emerge*. Understanding Holodynamics mobilizes the latent potential within people to better reach their personal and collective potential. This means holodynamists naturally tend to solve problems which are not solvable from other perspectives. They are able to make distinctions that provide greater degrees of freedom. This approach allows more effective and productive choices. This freedom is the basis of action that makes a real difference in building a future in which we can all unfold our greatest potential together.

You can hold the field:

Those who *hold the field* for others are Holodynamic Advocates. That is, those who sense the fullest potential of others and hold that potential as the primary reference for the other person are *holding a field* in which that potential is stimulated to emerge.

Assignment 6: Take a moment and imagine: what would life be like if, at some time in the future, this planet achieved a balanced state of being at its fullest potential? Write down what you imagine it would be like. Can you imagine what you would be doing that might be different than what you are doing now? Can you hold a field for this? What can you do today and in the near future that will make a difference? Outline.

This is why Chris Vlasaty Armata in Toronto, Canada established the Holodynamic Center for Body Balance. She has a staff and a network of medical doctors, psychologists and alternative medical practitioners who are trained in the Holodynamic view of reality, and they produce extraordinary results.

Perhaps this is why the Canadian government has asked the center to help Canadian cancer patients who everyone else has "given up on." Usually, they are shuffled away to die. Yet the clinic reports almost 95% of those patients have recovered. Using a combination of holistic approaches, Chris reports a research project now underway that isolates the use of Holodynamic processes as the primary healing influence in the healing process for cancer patients.

You can be certified. The principles and processes in this entire manual series are a *toolbox* that can be used to solve whatever problems we are facing in life. Like any other tools, these tools require both academic knowledge and specific skill development. People learn the materials. They become skillful in their applications. Learning this material is an educational process.

Since this is an educational process, the International Academy of Holodynamics provides certification at each level of development. The certification process takes each applicant, step by step, through the natural process of applying a specific approach to a field of information. These steps are called "The Circles of Success" in the academy.

CHAPTER THREE

CIRCLES OF SUCCESS

S UCCESS CAN BE ACHIEVED ONE STEP AT A TIME. IN BUSINESS SUCCESS IS MEASURED according to domains of responsibility. In the academy, these are referred to as *Circles of Success*. As participants learn to master one domain of information and the skills that are taught in that domain, they can be certified as competent and then they move on to the next circle.

There are seven Circles of Success. They can be outlined in brief as follows:

Circle One: **Advocate:** one who understands and advocates a Holodynamic view of life.

Circle Two: **Consultant**: a person who has the ability to track and transform holdynes.

Circle Three: **Facilitator**: one who can shift fields as in relive/prelive processes.

Circle Four: **Presenter**: a person who teams up and teach classes.

Circle Five: **Teacher**: one who can independently teach the entire series of classes.

Circle Six: **Masters**: a person who creates transformative projects.

Circle Seven: **Doctorate**: one who creates extraordinary results in both academic and practical matters using a Holodynamic approach.

In order to facilitate becoming a holodynamist and becoming the most effective teacher possible, it is recommended that you master each Circle of Success and learn to teach Holodynamics as a subject while you are applying it in your daily life. To understand a subject, apply it and then teach it is a natural process by which consciousness emerges about any subject. In this manual, we will approach the subject in a non-linear fashion. That is, we will teach the subject of Holodynamics, the science of it, so you can be an Advocate of Holodynamics. At the same time, you will learn how to apply it and teach it.

It is up to you to integrate it and facilitate this information into your state of being a Holodynamic Advocate. It becomes easy once you discover the enfolded dimensions of your own Full Potential Self. The Advocate inside of you is waiting to emerge. Thus, the first step is to access that state of being in which you *are* an Advocate.

What do I do in order to be successful within each Circle?

There are natural stages of development through which an Advocate must pass in order to become effective. Of course these same steps apply to becoming effective at anything whether it be as a person, a lover, in a career or even enlightened.

The first step is to recognize and "own" the Holodynamic nature of the universe.

Once you realize the universe is made of information, you also realize information is consciously structured. You can each structure your own version of reality. You can solve your problems, create a future in which we all can live and balance our ecology. You become an *Advocate*. Advocates recognize and take responsibility for their knowledge about the Holodynamic nature of reality. Advocates are proactive.

The second step is to learn specific principles and processes for unfolding potential.

Life is about unfolding potential. You learn to *consult* with others on how to potentialize their lives. You become a *Consultant*. Consultants are professionals who assist others in the application of the principles and processes of being aware of the whole dynamic of life. As a Consultant you have developed the ability to track holodynes. You teach the skills of accessing the enfolded dimensions of reality, transforming information systems and potentializing situations.

The third natural stage of development is to help groups of people understand the processes.

You will naturally begin to *facilitate* groups in potentialization. You will develop the skill to help others face their issues. You will share your information and hold a field for the unfolding of their personal potential and for the potential of your Holon. You learn to facilitate the shifting of information fields. You learn to access the past and the future and integrate that information into the present.

As you demonstrate your group skills ***you will naturally take the forth step and become a Presenter.***

Presenters team up with others, create and implement projects and teach formal classes in Holodynamics. You will be able to stand in front of assemblies of people who have come to learn the principles and processes of Holodynamics in order to make a difference in the world. Once you are seasoned in the processes and have met all the requirements, ***you will be able to take the fifth step and become a Teacher.*** You can be recognized and certified to teach Holodynamics as part of the community of Holodynamists. One by one you will learn about each enfolded dimension of reality and how to apply this information to solve complex problems. You will be able to teach this information to others.

Finally, as you move beyond the confines of your own district, you will find yourself teaching people from different cultures. You will find yourself taking on special projects and solving complex problems. When you do this you are taking the ***sixth step and becoming a***

Master of Holodynamics.

Within this Circle of Success you will find yourself becoming involved in transformation at every level. You will become adept at specific areas of interest. You may focus on environmental balance and develop new ways to manage pollution. You may develop a new battery that will make electric automobiles a viable realty. You may help end disease or eliminate poverty or end war. As you enter this arena you can be certified with a **Doctorate** from the International Academy of Holodynamics.

Each of the *manuals* in this series outlines in detail the context, content and teaching procedures within each Circle of Success. Thus the first manual is the **Advocate's Manual**, the second is the **Consultant's Manual**, the third is the **Facilitator's Manual**, the fourth is the **Presenter's Manual** and the fifth is the **Teacher's Manual.** The **Master's Manual** and the **Doctorate Manual** are yet to be written because they will be written by you in the actions you take.

By *taking the course* and meeting each of the certification requirements at each level, each Circle of Success meets international standards for excellence. When you have studied these materials and experienced their effectiveness in your personal life, you are more able to serve in the transformation of consciousness.

As an Advocate, you have *owned* your willingness to stand up for a view that includes the whole dynamic of reality and unfolds potential in every situation. You advocate focusing upon solutions, even to our most complex dynamics, and you are willing to share this information with others. In every way you advocate *taking the course* of your fullest possible potential in life.

Everyone who decides to advocate finding solutions (especially where none are evident) deserves our support. Such a decision reflects the future for life on earth. It's all about being *present*. This is one of the reasons we created a certification program and set the title of *ADVOCATE* for the first level of the *program on being present*. For more details on how to certify for each level of this program, see *Appendix A* at the back of this manual.

I cannot emphasize enough what a joy it is to walk this path with you and share this information. What follows is an attempt to outline the primary points of discovery for those who wish to become *present* and advocate to others to do the same.

BEING PRESENT

Being present means allowing your Full Potential Self to guide you in your life. It means you advocate reality. You experience the whole dynamic of life. You are Holodynamic.

As an advocate of reality you become a consultant of a healthy life; a facilitator of coherence through which each participant is able to integrate particle/rational thinking, wave/emotional dynamics and hyperspacial states of being into the harmonic power to manifest results. You become a presenter, a teacher and a master of the whole dynamic. Being present is contagious.

Being Present as an Advocate

An Advocate is one who advocates reality. The Advocate knows that life is about *the* emergence of the potential of self, others and life. The Advocate encourages others to take the course of being aligned with your Full Potential Self. Those who teach from the state of being at their Full Potential Self are able to encompass both the subject matter (academic content) and its emotional texture (the broader context*)* within still a larger dynamic (presence). This state of being present results in being able to find solutions to every problem facing the planet. Success is about operating within this larger dynamic.

Real solutions to real problems are found within *presence*. We have learned from both science and long experience that every problem is caused by its emerging potential solution. In other words, the problem shows up but the problem is only the symptom of an emerging potential. Those who *teach* actually advocate the emergence of the potential within every student and within every situation. Problems are opportunities to explore the emergence of potential.

Assignment 7: Organize your Holon into three sections. One part represents a linear approach to problem solving. A second part represents emotion or nonlinear approaches. A third represents presence.

Have the group design a situation in which a problem is presented.

Have part of the group use reason, a second part use emotion and a third demonstrating being present. Act out the problem. Discuss various effects. Record your summary in your journal.

You may someday get the chance to talk to Jeannie Low or Bobbie Barns from the Los Angeles area. These two teachers decided to put their Holodynamic skills to work when they took the challenge of getting gang members off the streets and back into school in the Los Angeles school districts.

Starting with about 300 drop-out students who were living on the streets of LA, their program grew to more than 600 participants within a few weeks. In one summer they were able to get every student back to academic standing.

How did they do it? The main ingredient was Holodynamic *presence*. How did then know what to do? They knew not only from deductive and inductive logic, not only from consensus of educators everywhere, but they knew from experiencing presence and inviting their students to do the same.

How did they experience presence? They facilitated presence by practicing solving complex problems. They found by actual experience that reality is Holodynamic. Everything is connected. Everything is conscious. Everything is driven by potential. Every problem is caused by its potential solution. Every Holodynamic teacher understands and attests to this reality. Such teachers are advocates of presence.

By now you will realize that it is my passion to help others become more dynamic and more interested in the whole dynamic of life. The new sciences of quantum physics, holographics and information theory, when integrated with the school of developmental psychology, are the best the world has to offer right now. Their findings are not absolute truths but they do provide an integrative language, a conceptual framework, if you will. This has proven to be a good vehicle for helping people understand what is happening when a teacher, a really *present* teacher, is holding a field for the unfolding of potential or the students.

Of course, you don't need to know all these new sciences to actually facilitate the unfolding of potential. It's just that knowing the new sciences helps with a more universal language by which people can understand what is happening when they go through such quantum leaps in consciousness.

Various schools of thought appear artificially separated, like parts of a body, just doing their own thing at a normal school system.

This series of manuals outlines the premises of the new sciences. They outline the basic skills for each step of the implicate order by which each person's own consciousness emerges. In these manuals I have adopt the new languages of the sciences into the language of the Advocate, Consultant, Facilitator, Presenter, Teacher, Master and Doctorate level. Each of these titles reflects an emerging step of consciousness. The manuals help build the basis for a new life view and a new education philosophy that helps build a more sustainable future.

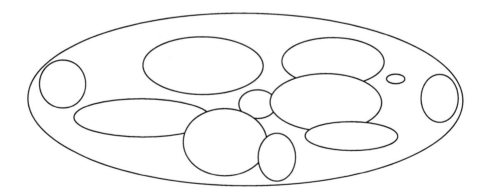

This new approach is an advantage in helping teachers and students more adequately manage the advent of the new Information Age, the sometimes overwhelming presence of computers and computer assisted education and everything else in this age of consciousness. There is an emerging realization that all information works together as one body. We just have to put the parts together.

Assignment 8: On the following page the parts of the diagram given on the previous page are reorganized. Was there any difference in the situation above, between linear, nonlinear and Holodynamic approaches? What, if any, were the differences?

Now look at the diagram on the following page. Is there any difference in the situation below, between the linear, non-linear and Holodynamics? What, if any, are the differences? Summarize your findings in your journal.

All information is part of one living body. All schools of thought, all religions, philosophies, sciences, governments and views of reality are one living, coherent information system.

How, for example, can education be personal, deep and experiential when complete courses, indeed, complete education tracks, are available simply by sitting down at a computer?

Students can learn subject matter as fast as they want, via personal, interactive computers. They can graduate from grade school, high school and university via computer-assisted courses at their own rate of progress.

How do we face the coming generation with assurance that students have, in fact, been educated to live *life* more fully? How do we assure that education prepares students to make a constructive contribution to community, to responsibly raise a family and help establish the next generation in a way that harmonizes with Nature and does not destroy life on the planet? These objectives can be assured only when both teachers and students become more Holodynamic. Advocates teach.

Assignment 9: Refer to M-Theory (see The Dance of Life, or refer to Stephen Hawking: The Universe in a Nutshell). *What similarities can be observed between what is being pre-*

sented in the material above and the formation of M-Theory? If any, list them in your journal.

CHAPTER FOUR

BEING THE TEACHER

ANY ADVOCATE IS A TEACHER. IT IS NATURAL. IT IS PART OF THE ESSENCE OF AN Advocate. It is like putting on a coat and finding yourself wrapped in the warmth of a new state of being. Anyone who advocates an expanded view of reality will naturally encourage others to find the information they need and help them create solutions to problems from within themselves. Once you begin to do this you become the teacher.

The Advocate/teacher knows that information cannot just be *poured into* a student. All information is already *within* each student. Education is a process of blending the information from the world outside with the information already contained within. This is done most effectively within the *context* of *presence*.

Students may learn content but they learn it better when it is experienced within a certain context. Content and context are retained and integrated better when they are nested in a larger framework, one which sets the stage for dynamic living from our fullest potential. From such a state of being, information pours *out* of the student. It is not so much pouring it *in*.

People have such natural curiosity they can find consensus, meaning, connection and character *within the information*. The first step, for the Advocate/teacher, is to recognize a common language. This means they must have the content clear in order to create the most effective teacher/student relationship possible.

The Content of Presence

This brings us to the first set of distinction made in the introductory courses of Holodynamics. The language of the new sciences gives us added accuracy in explaining the processes by which people can better reach their fullest potentials (which is the essence of education) and also can be used to show how you can access and use the Master Teacher within. The content of the classes comes from different branches of science. For example, you will want to know about the following branches of science.

Quantum physics allows distinctions regarding how consciousness functions in the human body and in collective intelligence.

Holographics helps everyone understand how memory is stored within the microtubules of every living cell and how everyday life is connected to parallel worlds through the quantum potential fields within each microtubule.

Information theory explains how information self-organizes and how information can be integrated within specific cultural and social belief systems.

When these sciences are applied to <u>developmental psychology</u>, a view of life emerges that allows a wider variety of distinctions and a more effective approach in meeting the challenges we face in life today.

This list goes on and on. There is wisdom in every school of thought and yet those who are trained in certain assumptions of the old schools sometimes have more resistance to change. Most of the old schools are embedded in their own event horizons and their holodynes keep them there even though their positions don't work anymore. Once exposed to the new, wider view of reality, people are more able to help others solve difficult problems in their personal lives and in the collective consciousness of society. But solutions are not even visible to people who are blinded by their old beliefs. The new sciences set new premises that free us in overcoming the old personal barriers to learning.

Students who learn the new sciences see the basis for change and they unfold their potential more easily. This unfolding provides natural motivation, self-discipline and an insatiable desire to discover. A teacher can facilitate this natural state of being by creating a *field* in which every student can unfold his or her fullest potential in life. The *teacher* recognizes the educational *process* and creates an environment in which students can explore and discover together the dimensions that will lead to success in life. Any Advocate can organize a study group. Any Advocate can create a Holon and open up the doors to a new future.

These advances are not possible using the old, mechanistic sciences of the 17th century or through ancient cultural and religious belief systems. This is a new age and the new information is available. This information is needed now. Our school systems have failed to reach anywhere near their potential. Most schools are 20 years behind the information wave. We are using processes that squeeze out more than 30 percent of our students before they graduate. We are emptying our schools and filling up our prisons and mental treatment facilities at an alarming rate. This is an age in which new levels of consciousness are available and are necessary. This is why we teach Holodynamics.

Assignment 10: List the reasons that linear thinking limits success. What is the value of linear thinking? Discuss. Record your major points in your journal.

Assignment 11: How do you feel about passion? In what ways are emotional dynamics limited? Discuss. Record your major points in your journal.

Consistent with this approach is the necessity of setting the stage so that the information is made available with as much effectiveness as possible. This can only be done when the teacher is *present* with the students. Being *present* is more than understanding the academic subject (although it helps to make the subject reasonable and more understandable). What I am saying here is that it must be more than a presentation of information in a reasonable and logical fashion. It is even more than demonstrating emotional support and love (although this also helps to deliver the message with feeling and conviction). It includes reason and positive regard and more. It is being *present*.

41

Assignment 12: How does Presence make a difference? Why is Presence necessary in education? Discuss and record your observations.

Once we become aware that we can teach with Presence, the question becomes, "How does a person actually teach when they are present?" Beginning with quantum physics, four new premises have immediate application.

Teaching using Four Premises of Quantum Physics

There are at least four premises of quantum physics that have impacted the world view of reality. Such principles allow us to better understand what is happening in life. These four basic premises are as follows: *Every set of circumstances is driven by potential; everything is made of information in motion which manifests in three ways: particles (linear), waves (non-linear, emotional) and being (conscious, creative integrated presence); there is an implicate order; and everything is connected.*

1. Every set of circumstances is driven by potential

Part of the reason quantum physicists have come to this conclusion is that matter *does not exist until something gives it form.* A single photon, for example, takes on the form of a particle or wave depending upon whether it is being *measured* as a particle or wave. In a very practical way, experiments at the subatomic level show that photons, or particles of light that make up all matter, only take on form when they are measured to have form.

Electrons, for example, exist only as *potential* until they are given form. Since everything is made of subatomic particles, such as photons and electrons, it can also be said that nothing exists except as potential until it is given form. It follows that every set of circumstances in life exists only as potential until it is given form.

Once this basic premise is understood, then it follows that *every situation in life exists only as potential until it is given form.* What you and I experience in life actually emerges from the field of potential because life is being *caused* to emerge. This is basic to understanding what is real in this world.

Each photon is *driven* to take on form according to the measurement being used (for example, a single slit or double slit). If it is a single slit that is used to measure the photon, it becomes a particle. If it is a double slit is used, the photon becomes a wave.

Until it is measured, it has no specific location but only the potential for a location. It will, however, take on both its form and location once the measurement is provided. This same dynamic seems to occur in the formation of life. Once energy, flux and non-linearity exist, *life emerges* (see Prigogene).

Since every set of circumstances exists only as potential, we can say every set of circumstances is dependent on, or driven by, its potential. This same law applies to humans. *Thus every person is driven by his or her Full Potential Self.*

It is also scientifically consistent that *all situations have a potential that is waiting to emerge.* The form that matter *takes* depends upon the form it is *given*. What gives it form? Who decides? What causes matter to emerge? What drives you and me?

In order to understand these questions we must turn to the science of holographics. From holographics it becomes obvious that *consciousness determines the form*. *We* get to choose. Thus choice, including how consciousness functions, the games people play, and the emerging implicate orders of consciousness, are central themes in each Holodynamic course.

Most people want to solve their problems. The choice to view a certain set of circumstances as "a problem" is part of the process by which the dynamics take on the form of "problems." When one realizes that every problem is caused by its emerging solution, one's view of the dynamics changes. Solutions become the form.

Any set of circumstances can be viewed as an emerging potential. Focusing on the emerging potential leads to the emergence of the solution because *every problems is caused by its potential solution.* This change of focus, from *problems* to *emerging potential solutions,* allows a person to become part of the solution to problems and thus to become more effective in every aspect of life.

How do we know? How does any responsible person *know?* There are several processes that are used in order for people to know anything. Here are a few:

a. We can look at the evidence and then use two kinds of processes for exploring the evidence: **deductive** or **inductive logic.** This is the scientific method used to explore whether something can be shown to be false. We can set up experiments and test our theories. Our experiments can be "outward and upward" or "downward and inward" experiments. This leads to deductive or inductive, logical conclusions. We can replicate and retest each theory, always looking for a better explanation of what appears to be real. This is the heart of science. We can know from deductive or inductive logic.

b. We can tell from the **implications** of science. For example, the first principle of quantum physics implies that every set of circumstances is driven by potential. Thus, by implication, we can know that every problem is driven by its potential solution.

c. We can also tell from **consensus**. People agree on certain things. We believe, for example that there are laws of nature that are in harmony with what we experience. There are people who make their life study the study of natural laws. There are people who study human behavior, and myriads of other subjects and all these people are in coherence about consensus. There is a general consensus within all schools of thought. We know from consensus that solutions to problems are inherent within the problem.

d. We also know because **it works.** People solve problems and manifest potential in arenas where nothing else seems to work. In other words, we know because we can ex-perience it directly.

These methods of knowing what is real - the inductive-deductive scientific method, by implication, by consensus or by practical functioning - are helpful but there is more to knowing than these methods. Knowing is multidimensional. *There are other dimensions* involved in how you know something is true.

It does not matter whether the set of the circumstance is you, personally, your loved ones, family, friends, the workplace or the planet. Every set of circumstances, good or bad, safe or dangerous, productive or destructive, it is all driven by potential. Knowing what is real or what is true comes from within the quantum potential field.

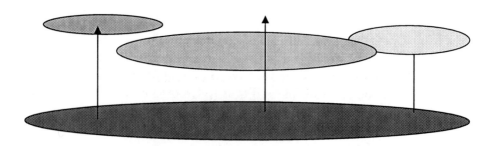

**Every set of circumstances in life
Is driven by potential**

What potential drives your life? The potential of *you* drives you and every set of circum-stances of your life. When you align with your Full Potential Self, you are *present* and you know what is real. Presence is the key to living your life, finding your mission and understanding meaning and enjoying everything. Being present is the most powerful way of knowing anything.

This manual teaches how to facilitate each participants' personal experience in becom-ing *present*, experiencing a new, fresh and effective approach to life by discovering his or her personal potential and giving it form.

We call this the Full Potential Self. It comes from a *Holodynamic state of being*. "Taking the course" means to develop a personal relationship with one's Full Potential Self. It is about learning to use the information from the Full Potential Self to guide you in your daily living and committing to this specific course of action. This commitment provides an all-empowering state of being in which anyone can emerge to their fullest capabilities.

Focusing on the Full Potential Self

If you were building a house, you would want to make sure it had a good foundation. As an Advocate/teacher, you will want to make sure that your information has a good foundation. People will need to know how they can know. Focusing on their Full Potential Self opens the door to a whole new dimension so they can know for themselves what is real and how to solve any type of problem. Here are some ways to open the door to their fullest, best possible self.

What do you want?

Questions such as "What do you want?" can be used as a reflection of that potential within a person. Their potential is trying to manifest. It wants to emerge. How people perceive their self, or life or their place in life, *gives form* to their potential. These "exploring questions" allow them to step back, look at their wants and visions, and bring this potential into their consciousness.

Holodynamists will not take self-perception too seriously during this stage of exploration because wants and visions can be dominated by holodynes, memories, other people's values, inherited beliefs and any number of other factors. The student is usually unable to distinguish between their real potential and these other information systems. It is enough for now to *get a reading* on the state of consciousness to which each student is attuned. You can tell which p-brane (Townsend) they are using and this can be a vital step on the path to potentializing.

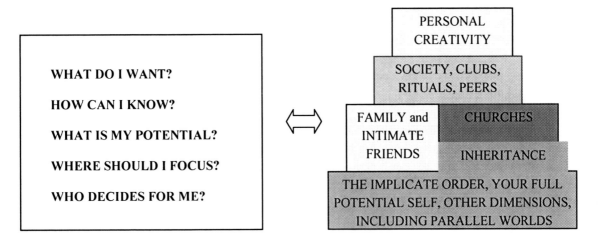

Assignment 13: Outline how you "know" what is real? What is your reference for know-

ing? Do you really want to take responsibility for the knowing of your own potential? If so, where do you start? How do you know you won't be distracted or thrown off course by other influences? Discuss and outline in detail in your journal.

Imagine a Place of Peace:

By focusing your imagination upon a Place of Peace, you begin to take control of your internal world. By using your senses of sight, sound, smell, taste and touch lets you imagine what it would be like to be in a place where everything is peaceful. You create an internal information field that establishes your own personal state of being at peace. You stop all the interference and create a field of acceptance.

When you write it down and share your Place of Peace with others, you set the field so at any time you can choose to be in a peaceful state of mind. Not only does this come in handy during moments of stress or crisis (like when you are driving on the freeway and someone cuts in front of you), but it sets up a precedent in which your state of being at peace becomes self-sustaining.

What this means is that in your personal life the holographic dimension of reality responds accordingly. If you are at war within yourself, those around you will respond with war games. When you are at peace within yourself, those around you will respond more peacefully.

Assignment 14: Create a Place of Peace. Describe your Place of Peace in your journal. Share this information with someone else.

Imagine your Full Potential Self:

One of the most powerful experiences a person can have is to discover the potential that drives them. This discovery can be more powerful than any addiction, mental illness or social disease. It has proven, over and over, to be potentially more powerful than any other single event in a person's life.

One process for facilitating the discovery of your Full Potential Self is to imagine, while in your Place of Peace, that your Full Potential Self is coming toward you. It's that simple. Imagine it, sense it. What are you like at your very best? Use all your senses. Call in the full perceptive powers of your amazing biological, holographic sensory system. Open up the door to your hyperspacial counterpart.

Do you understand that it is possible for everyone to meet their Full Potential Self in person, to have a daily, interactive relationship that is both a source of assurance and a state of shared being?

Can you feel the love and caring from your Full Potential Self? Can you discern the qualities which make up the **real** essence of yourself?

Opening yourself to this dimension of reality can be one of the great discoveries of your entire life. I say the "real" essence of yourself because, from a quantum perspective, your personal **potential** is *more real* than the holographic projection of your physical body. It is more real than your psychological personality, your relationships, systems, or even your principled position in life.

Why do I refer to the Full Potential Self as a "holographic projection"? We will explore why this view has become so widely accepted in more detail later in these manuals. You will soon realize that once you discover the potential that is driving you, the next question you will usually ask is, "Why do I have to go through all the difficulties of my life?"

The answer for you comes *from* your Full Potential Self. As soon as you access this dimension all the usual data about your inner Self or selves, psychological traits and the thousands of books written about the subject become simple reflections of your Full Potential Self. Your Full Potential Self is the source of every situation in your life.

Assignment 15: Communicate with your Full Potential Self. Listen. Are there any messages? How does your Full Potential Self feel about you? Are you willing to establish an ongoing relationship? Record your findings.

2. Everything is made of information in motion that manifests in three ways: particle, wave and presence

Your body has a complex information exchange system. Each cell, every organ and all body parts have the ability to both receive and transmit information. Each sub-system carries its own specific information management system.

Your eye, for example, has a complex information processing system. It contains-

(a) the FOVEA, which is a pin dot concentration of rods at the back of the retina. The fovea is receptive to particle information. When the fovea is destroyed, the eye cannot register specific information. You cannot, for example, read the letters on a page if your fovea isn't working;

(b) the PERIPHERY, or lining of the retina, which is composed mainly of cones and from all indications, takes in the entire context of the information. This provides the basis for reference waves within the holographic dynamic of consciousness; and

(c) the OPTIC NERVE that receives, transforms and transmits the information.

How, then, does the eye perceive what is going on? This is where the science of holographics helps. The periphery provides the context framework for perception. The fovea provides the specific content. In Holographics the wave reference (context) and the particle reference (content) are the basic ingredients for the creation of a three dimensional hologram.

In a similar way, the eye provides the basics for three-dimensional images that we see through our eyes. This process is holographic. The particle and wave information is processed within the optic nerve where it is transformed by a Gaborian type of transform (used to transform three-dimensional images) into quantum frequencies that travel through the microtubule systems into the memory storage system of the body as holodynes.

In *The Dance of Life,* we discuss in more detail the holographic dimension of consciousness. As it turns out, there are many dimensions to consciousness. It is not the eye that actually *sees* the beauty in a flower or the ear that actually *hears* the music. Art, music and dance are typical peripheral experiences (wave dynamics) in which one can sense the "motion of the ocean" or the "magic of the music." But this sense of things does not come from the physical body alone. It comes from a much more complex and fascinating aspect of presence.

We can see how wave functions are an integral part of our perception process and we also will discuss how facts and linear logic are managed within our linear perception processes. Information can be received and processed in a linear, logical manner. It can also be processed in a wave, emotional process. But we embrace both of the linear and the wave processes with our integrative state of conscious *presence.* It's within this larger context that everything begins to make sense.

All of our senses are composed of holographic screens (Pribram) that are orchestrating a multidimensional conscious presence. Everything we think and feel, as well as everything we experience, is connected intimately to hyperspace and to our Full Potential Self.

Assignment 16: What are three distinctive processes by which information organizes? How do differences among people are related to different information processing patterns? How does the information given above provide an advantage when it comes to resolving these differences? Write your observations in your journal and discuss your thoughts among yourselves in your Holon.

3. There is an implicate order

Enfolded within the fabric of reality is an implicate order. This enfolded order seems to guide the emergence of consciousness. In other words, we each grow more mature in our lives because the quantum potential field within provides us with a built-in maturation process.

This order manifests in both a linear and non-linear manner. It is specific and non-specific, local and non-local. It is physical and non-physical at the same time. Consciousness can be observed as it manifests in the body. One aspect of this can be seen at the center of each microtubule where it appears as a quantum potential field of disorganized water. It is here, within the center of the microtubules, that consciousness begins to emerge.

The first level of organization appears as spinners within the quantum potential field. These spinners show up everywhere. They can be seen in the creation of the DNA. They can be seen in the formation of electrons. They are also found within the water of your microtubules.

When they show up in the microtubules, some very interesting things can be seen as happening. From out of these spinners emerge single strands of water molecules coming from the quantum potential fields and extending into more complexity as they reach the inner wall of the microtubule. This process of spinning out of hyperspace and into the fluid media of the water, is a process of hierarchical order. The water molecules form into holodynes.

Holodynes from Hyperspace:

Holodynes become self-organizing information systems. It seems to be a built-in order. Information from hyperspace seems to form from out of the quantum potential field into spinners of information that run along single strands of water molecules. They feed directly into multidimensional holographic images. The water is the media. Its molecules organize into multi-dimensional dynamic holograms.

These holodynes are evidently held in place by the dimer molecules that make up the wall of the microtubules. Holodynes are conscious *entities* (or self-organizing information systems) that have the power to cause things to happen. Herein lays the source of intelligent action that can be seen organizing the biological and mental functions of the body and brain.

Holodynes from Environment:

At the same time, we live in a physical environment. Information is being received by our physical senses, such as the eye, ear, etc., and is being fed into the microtubules, where it is stored in the form of holodynes and correlates itself with what is already in storage. The environmental impact of your daily life experiences is part of the information system of your consciousness. It's not one or the other. Both hyperspace and physical space are involved at the same time.

Holodynes as Transmitters:

This system also has the ability to transmit its information. Holodynes are quantum. They give off frequencies that transmit their information throughout the body and beyond.

This receiving-storing-transmitting system is a two-way feedback loop where information being projected from hyperspacial dimensions is being correlated with information being fed from our physical senses into the microtubules. The integration process is holographic, dynamic and fluid. At the center of this system are holodynes.

Long Term Memory:

Holodynes direct the microtubules so that the valence patterns of the dimer switches (molecules that make up the wall of the microtubules) can maintain the form of the holodynes.

The holodynes become stable. The dimer switches grow arms (Microtubule Associated Protein Strings or MAPS). MAPS grow at exactly the frequency cross over points and thus assist in maintaining certain frequency coordinates over time. This is referred to as *long-term memory*. This process of becoming stable is what helps to build a communication system that eventually controls human behavior patterns through which our consciousness emerges.

Assignment 17: List at least five mechanisms that are essential in the creation of memory. Why is memory storage important? Discuss.

Holodynes can be seen creating cell division (mitosis), controlling biochemistry, managing neural activity and creating coherence throughout the body. Holodynes also create the pathologies we experience as humans. This includes not only our diseases, mental illnesses and personal consciousness, but also our collective consciousness. Holodynes are causal in our relationships, social systems, businesses, political systems and our entire relationship with Nature.

Assignment 18: Discuss the evidence for each function of holodynes. How do we know this is true? What difference does this information make in everyday life? What can be done about holodynes that are dysfunctional?

What is helpful is to understand the natural order by which holodynes can mature, change their form and become healthy. This applies to individuals and it also applies to the collective community.

It is interesting to know that consciousness is not limited to a single body but can also be observed as collective consciousness. Just as the quantum frequencies create coherence within the body, similar frequencies also create collective coherence. What this means is that all our pathologies and the inhumanities we heap upon each other and upon Nature - our destructive wars, greed, hate, and all other forms of pathos - are *transformable*. Furthermore, this transformation occurs according to a natural, built-in order.

Transformation:

Transformation is implicate. It is contained within the information systems that are being projected from hyperspace. The most comprehensive outline of the emergence of the implicate order of consciousness is outlined in brief in the text *Holodynamics* (1990) and is briefed in the chart on *the Stages of Development* (see *The Dance of Life*). This chart provides a general outline of how intelligence and consciousness unfolds individually, among one's holodynes, within the body and mental functions, and collectively.

We realize now that information cannot be limited to this space-time continuum. Information travels hyperspacially, faster than the speed of light and is connected to parallel dimensions. We live on a two-way street where communication is both coming from and going into hyperspace.

The good news, even the *great* news, is that all information systems follow a similar implicate order in their own growth. Once understood, the implicate order can be consciously used to change the physics of holodynes and transform them from immature stages of development into mature stages. This is accomplished by the process called *tracking;* in which people are able to access holodynes and allow them to unfold their fullest potential by guiding them through the stages of their own natural development.

Think about it. Everything in life follows an order of growth. What could possibly be strange about information systems following an order of growth? Once the possibility is realized, the evidence shows it is not only a probability but a reality. The only question that remains is: Are we willing to care enough to reach in and connect, and follow through enough to make a difference?

Assignment 19: Review the chapter on quantum computers in The Dance of Life and relate this information to how one person can possibly make a difference.

4. Everything is connected

Physicists talk about the network of dualities that make up the fabric of space. Everything is connected in some dimension of reality and, even though some of us may not be aware of this connection, our lack of awareness does not mean it does not exist. Everything is connected whether we agree by consensus or not.

We have seen that within our microtubules is a quantum potential field that is capable of communication beyond the speed of light. We have observed that birds, insects and schools of fish are capable of collective action that does not require a space-time medium.

We have presented this information from high-speed cameras, which show it takes 1/70 of a second for an individual bird to perceive a predatory hawk and register this perception within its microtubules. It takes an additional 1/70 of a second for the bird to react. The interesting fact is that all birds in the flock react in the last 1/70 of a second even though only one bird saw the hawk. The other birds did not need to see the hawk. They got the message hyperspacially.

This phenomenon is called "swarm" intelligence (Kevin Kelly). Swarm intelligence is a form of *collective consciousness* and becomes much more understandable when we look through our holographic glasses.

Holographically, we communicate with each other via our microtubules. Our holodynes give off quantum frequencies that travel via hyperspace. That's why birds and bees can swarm as flocks. It's also why humans develop great cities and also why they go to war. Collective consciousness is a quantum phenomenon. It occurs when information and energy exchanges are created within our microtubules. The holodynes within our microtubules are connected to everyone else's holodynes. All consciousness is connected.

Assignment 20: Discuss what difference collective consciousness makes. What would happen if we did not have collective consciousness? What chance do we have to survive as a species if our collective consciousness becomes self-destructive? Is the collective of the human race isolated from the collective of Nature? Can this collective be transformed? If so, how? Record your thoughts.

The application of these four premises leads to transformation. Transformation is spontaneous. It is the reorganization of information systems according to the unfolding of their own potential. This changing-of-form is natural. It is part of the dance of life and you and I are central to that dance. We have the ability to be consciously present and to place ourselves in a conscious context that can help create a more sustainable future.

PRESENCE AS CONTEXT

Context refers to the learning *environment*. How does information take on meaning, find application and become part of the dynamics of consciousness? Particle information must have a contextual field, or a reference wave, into which it fits. Movie-makers, musicians, artists and dancers understand context. Another way to say this is that the context gives emotional meaning to any situation. Presence must also have a contextual framework.

Holodynamics, for example, provides a dynamic context in which participants explore, practice and apply the premises in a context which provides meaning. It was in the context that Brad, mentioned above, found meaning to the tragedy of his life. It was in context that military leaders of the Soviet Union found new vision beyond war. It is within context that people who are diseased find health.

In order to understand the context, we will explore each principle of quantum physics from its context framework.

Premise one: Every set of circumstances is driven by potential

The context for this premise lies in the discovery of one's Full Potential Self. The Full Potential Self provides, as a living, dynamic being, the context for everything that happens in the course of a person's life. People are guided by and find their solutions to problems within the context of their personal Full Potential Self. "Unfolding Potential" becomes an adventure guided by one's Full Potential Self.

In addition, your Place of Peace becomes a context tool by which you can immediately access the holodynes that are influencing your consciousness. Then, in the context of alliance with your Full Potential Self, you can access the quantum state of coherence, connect to swarm intelligence, collective consciousness and discover the solutions to every problem.

In this context, problems become opportunities for unfolding potential solutions. Problems are viewed as being caused by their potential solutions and orchestrated by your Full Potential Self. Every experience of life becomes an adventure. Those experiences that once were tragic, traumatic and negative are considered as part of the vacation from knowing.

Assignment 21: Since everything is driven by potential, how does this change the framework through which you view reality? How does this change effect how you look at problems?

Premise two: Everything is made of energy that manifests as particle, wave or presence.

There are particles, waves, and presence in every thought processes. When a holodyne uses a particle framework, it processes its information in a linear way. When that holodyne takes over a person's consciousness, the person thinks in a linear, rational and sequential manner.

On the other hand, when a holodyne that is using a wave orientation to process its information takes charge of the person's consciousness, the person's framework changes. He becomes an emotional, non-linear, feeling person. The holographic screens that cover the person's senses change. The person's view of reality becomes quantum.

When the holodynes involved are mature and can embrace particle and wave dynamics at the same time, the person become present. From this framework, the consciousness of the person changes into an intuitive, integrative, solution oriented, knowing and creative being. In such a state, this person becomes part of the solution to the problems we are facing in today's world. This is why we advocate Holodynamics.

We know that holodynes are formed from both experiential input and creative imagination. They are also inherited from genetic sources that are handed down from generation to generation. They also can be sourced from the quantum potential field directly into the micro-tubules and can be housed collectively and passed on via family and cultural modeling. We are part of a multidimensional reality.

The significance of this context can be demonstrated through simple role playing. Role playing allows common situations, which could easily be solved, to be set up in a classroom. During the role playing, holodynes can be seen actually taking over the situation and often making solutions seem impossible. It is also possible to demonstrate the transformation process by tracking the holodynes and then replaying the role to demonstrate that solutions are always possible.

Assignment 22: How does the context of different information processing patterns affect holodynes? How does context relate to how people think, feel and behave? What difference does this information make when it comes to the process of transforming holodynes? Can holodynes be transformed without accessing the source of the holodynes? Discuss and write notes in your journal.

Premise three: There is an implicate order

Each form of life has a built-in growing pattern. In this context, consciousness has a built-in order by which it emerges. I spent a major part of my life researching every branch of knowledge available so that I could learn everything possible about this implicate order of consciousness.

The *Stages of Development* chart is the combination of each "outward and upward" and "downward and inward" scientific research available. In other words, this chart is a summary of the best information available from every branch of science, religion, education and philosophy about consciousness. In this context, once the implicate order of consciousness was outlined for humans, it was a natural step to investigate whether a similar order applied to holodynes. This was tested and confirmed. Thus, the process of tracking was born.

What is this implicate order of consciousness? The first level of manifestation is physical. People must have bodies in order for personality, relationships, systems, principles and universal states of being to manifest. Within the physical dimension are many sub-levels of growing environments or, as Rupert Sheldrake suggests, "morphogenic fields" in which each stage creates an environment in which the next stage forms.

A similar growth order exists within each stage of development. Personality forms according to sub-stages in which morphogenic fields create the next stage of manifestation of human intelligence, moral character, values and ethics. Intelligence *grows* according to this built-in order.

Relationships likewise develop. They emerge from the implicate order and are given form each time we make a choice. We sculpture our relationships. We can choose to feed and nurture them or they can die of neglect or abuse.

These same growth patterns are evident in systems, manifestation of principles and universality. All six levels and all their subsystems grow according to an implicate order.

Once this order is better understood, a single holodyne can be accessed (under the guidance of one's Full Potential Self), invited into a morphogenic field, which induces its next stage of development (within the context of a field of love), and then invited to explore its own potential.

Once the holodyne obtains information about its own potential, this new information becomes part of its own spontaneous transformation. Holodynes grow according to the same order and within the same processes as humans except they do not seem to have an investment in time. They can mature instantaneously.

In this way, the context for every set of circumstances can be identified as part of the whole dynamic. No matter what or where, the entire situation is driven by some potential that can be accessed, aligned with and utilized to unfold the potential solution for that situation.

Assignment 23: List five significant findings regarding the implicate order and explain

why each finding is significant.

Premise Four: Everything is connected

There is a series of relationships in physics called *dualities,* which demonstrate that everything is made of one, interconnected dynamic field of potential. What this implies is that every situation, including every other person, is inherently connected to me and you. There is no separation. From this context, anything that teaches separation is an illusion.

This means that, in reality, there are no pyramids of power. There is no basis for religious or political differences; there is no justification for war or division among races or nations. While it is true that we humans play a series of games in life, all games are chosen and everyone's Full Potential Self is in coherence with everyone else's. This view provides a different context from which to look at the games that people play.

Understanding that, in some dimension, everything is connected allows you to realize that when a game is being played, everyone involved has agreed to play. The challenges we face in life are all part of the agreement we have made. We are living *under covenant.*

The Covenant:

The challenges we face are held in place by why I call "the Covenant." The Covenant is a field of information that exists because of an agreement made outside of time and space. When we discovered this dimension and began to explore it, we found the Covenant is dynamic. It can be changed. We can shift the entire field.

Not only that, but in order to unfold a given potential in our own life, it is often necessary to *shift the entire field.* It's part of the challenge we face. Can we become conscious of the whole dynamic so that we can unfold our fullest potential in a specific dynamic? Can we become aware of the larger picture so we can align our piece of the puzzle with the whole?

This series of courses covers in detail the processes that have been developed for field shifting. We can shift our fields here, in this life, and we can also enter into parallel dimensions and transform those holodynes that are influencing us here.

The diagram that follows is a depiction of the constant influence of parallel worlds on every aspect of consciousness. If you will follow the numbering, the diagram reads as follows:

(1)Information coming from these hyperspacial dimensions is (2) brought into coherence by the Full Potential Self of each person or of each life form. (3) This information reflects the hidden order or implicate order (4) coming from hyperspacial dimensions. This information is then transmitted directly into the quantum potential field and given form as holodynes (5).

Holodynes, in turn, are encased within the protective cover of the microtubules. (6) Microtubules are small tubes that weave the very fabric of every cell. The walls of microtubules are made of rings of 13 molecules called "spiners" that open and close. When the spiner molecule is open it has a positive valence. When it is closed it has a negative valence and when it is *in between* (neither open nor closed) its valence changes to neutral. In some way then spiners hold the information fields in place something like the mainframe memory in a computer.

This complex memory system of the spinner walls of microtubules somehow allows the holodynes within the microtubules to remain stable and also to become self-organizing. They exhibit the characteristics of self-organizing information systems (7) and have the power to cause things to happen.

For example, the wall of the microtubule grows *arms* called Microtubule Associated Protein String (MAPS) that control the biochemistry of the body. If the body needs a certain substance, the *MAPS* can be seen reaching out, selecting the substance needed from the bloodstream, and passing it along until it reaches its desired destination. MAPS deposit the substance exactly where it is needed.

Furthermore, microtubules exhibit a quantum frequency (8) that resonates throughout the body. These frequencies are called *Frohlech frequencies* because they were predicted by Herbert Frohlech in 1962. These frequencies are quantum because they resonate at subatomic levels and do not seem to be limited to space or time (9), which are not shown in the diagram.

Frohlech frequencies seem to have many functions but one of the most interesting is that they control the neural networks of the body (10), including the learning hierarchies and instinctive behavior (11). They can be seen controlling cellular construction (12) and mitosis and it is totally consistent to assume they are instrumental in the construction and design of DNA and RNA that are passed on through the sperm and the egg during reproduction.

The resonating frequencies of the quantum dynamics of microtubules (as coded within the holodynes) are also responsible for control of the fine-grained and gross-grained screens of our body senses. From all indications, holodynes control all body functions (13). This would account for the primary cause of diseases and even the rapid changes in thought and feelings that make life so interesting.

Gaining access and a greater measure of control on your holodynes means that you can also control your holographic screens. Thus what you see, hear, touch, taste and smell will change according to the holodynes that are in control at any given moment in time. Each holodyne gives off a specific series of quantum frequencies. Everyone has different holodynes and thus everyone's experience with life takes on a unique, individual. This is why we have so many differences among humans.

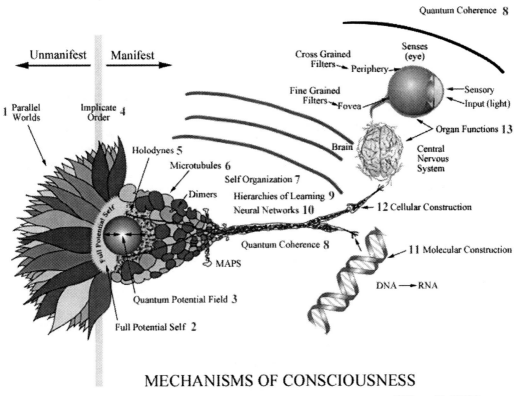

MECHANISMS OF CONSCIOUSNESS

V. Vernon Woolf 1999
©All Rights Reserved

Parallel Worlds send information through the Full Potential Self into the Quantum potential fields in the microtubules, through holodynes into the body and into the field of information of the collective consciousness.

Assignment 24: How many mechanisms of consciousness can you identify? How many are you able to access?

Our holodynes also transmit the information via Frohlech frequencies into the information fields of the collective. This is what causes swarm intelligence and collective consciousness. This is why one person can impact the entire community. We give off a resonating frequency that is picked up in a quantum field. It also means that to transform a single holodyne is to change the physics of the worlds.

Any change that can be orchestrated in a holodyne by a person will create a rippling effect that creates a corresponding change within the collective. This is called field shifting.

Assignment 25: What evidence is there that "the Covenant" actually exists? Discuss and make notes.

Assignment 26: What is "field shifting"? Does shifting a field have any potential affect on anything? If so, what is the potential effect? How does the above information provide a context for change? Discuss in your Holon.

Your Family Tree:

In Holodynamics, we begin the process of field shifting by focusing upon the field of the participant's family tree. Family holodynes are some of the most powerful holodynes governing a participant's life. In order to shift these fields, it is necessary to access the holodynes of the entire family tree. We explore how the holodynes of the family tree are passed on from generation to generation and create an environment in which they can transform into their fullest possible potential.

Thus it is possible to *access the causal dynamics involved in family dysfunction* and, using the Place of Planning, it becomes possible to access the collective consciousness of everyone's Full Potential Self. This Holodynamic approach also gives us access to parallel worlds where we can use their guidance to identify and transform the entire field. Such field-shifting creates dynamic results in the lives of family members - even those who are not aware of the processes.

In this way, any problem faced by individuals, communities, countries and the planet can be seen in an entirely new light. We live in a multidimensional world. Every situation is intimately interwoven with our experience on earth and it is also connected to parallel worlds at the same time. What this means is that any problem is an invitation to discover its hidden purpose and unfold its potential.

Assignment 27: Create a Genogram of your family tree. Identify what you know about each person in your family tree. What patterns have been passed on from generation to generation in your family? Discuss what you can do to shift the field of your family tree. Make notes.

PRESENCE and RESULTS

When you are faced with a specific situation, whatever context you use will determine the approach you take and this will create the results you get. When you are present, you will naturally encourage the unfolding of the hidden potential within each set of circumstances. This is a choice for *updrafting* and giving life to the situation. You will get better results. Other approaches will *downdraft* and cause the further death of the situation. Different contexts get different results. Presence gets the best results.

Once aware of the hyperspacial connection you have with the living universe, it becomes possible to be more present in your daily interactions with others. You can tell the difference between updraft and downdraft choices. Once aware of the reality of the Full Potential Self of every person, you become aware of the *covenant* with each other to help each other create what they want in their lives. It's an embracive context.

The Covenant takes place in hyperspace. You can understand it by visiting the Place of Planning. If you want more energy, health, abundance, self-esteem, creativity, intimacy, synergy with others, more integrity, knowing oneness or whatever, you can utilize the premises and processes of Holodynamics, access the Place of Planning and get the desired results. Others can do the same. We are the creative artists that sculpture the future of this planet.

As each one of us get closer and closer, according to the natural implicate order by which results are obtained, we can support each other in the transformation of our holodynes and shift our field dynamics so that the potential can emerge in its desired form.

In order to understand how this can be done, I would like you to look at the four premises of quantum physics and come to realize that when these premises are applied to practical situations people get better results.

PREMISE ONE produces internal validation, overcoming of dependency relationships - including drug and other substance abuse, diseases and all forms of physical limitations.

PREMISE TWO produces personal confidence, transforming fears, hatred, insecurity and all forms of self-defeating behaviors into genuine confidence and creative initiative.

PREMISE THREE produces transformation of holodynes, relationships and empowering of entire system to reach the synergistic potential.

PREMISE FOUR produces integrity with all of life and a sense of being one with all dimensions of realty. It produces a practical, dynamic incentive for extending one's initiative into the living oneness of the universe and allows all participants to touch the lives of everyone in their past and future and in parallel worlds as well.

There is no love greater than that love which touches all dimensions of reality with the healing, knowing and universal presence of one's Full Potential Self.

Within this context and with this specific content, it becomes possible for us, as a group of individuals, to present to the world a uniform series of courses and an association of holodynamists, who can be of great service in shifting the field in a Holodynamic way. We have formalized this movement into the International Academy of Holodynamics and we invite you to join with us.

What follows is the current curriculum of the International Academy of Holodynamics for empowering potential personally and internationally. All Advocate/Teachers have agreed that this body of information, including the content and context, the principles and processes, that are known as *Holodynamics*. What follows is the Introductory, *Phase I* course in Holodynamics, which is entitled *Unfolding Potential.*

We recognize that each Teacher will have creative ideas and a variety of processes and materials that might be included in the Phase I Unfolding Potential Course in Holodynamics. In order to keep the content and context similar and to build an international entity for the course, we have agreed to present recommended changes to a group of Master Teachers within the Master's Council. Once demonstrated and approved, these new suggestions can be incorporated into the courses and included in this manual so that everyone will be able to teach this new material in the future.

One look at the future is worth more than the entire content of the books written about the future. One glimpse óf the Master Teacher you *are* is worth more than all the influence you could possibly get from others. One twinkle of the eye can carry more meaning than meaning itself. May the love we are and the choices we make, lead us to unfolding the greatest potential possible, and help create a future that we choose.

The course outline that follows is only a suggested outline. It works and it has been distilled from a variety of approaches. It is a tool for those who wish to teach or share Holodynamics as a subject.

We have outlined the basic principles and processes that are the heart of the Holodynamic Phase I introductory course. The real teaching, that state of being from which new information is manifest, comes from the field you and your team set for each course. It comes from the participants as well. I hope you enjoy using these tools. It is the touch of the Master's hand that allows the geni-us to emerge in everyone.

Assignment 28: Review the premises of quantum physics. Discuss these with your Holon. Practice their application. For example, pick a situation from your past that was difficult for you to handle. Review back in time and remember as many details as possible. How would understanding and applying the basic premises outlined above, have changed the situation? Discuss and demonstrate for your group.

CHAPTER FIVE

A COURSE ON POTENTIALIZING

Introduction:

THERE IS NO WAY TO STOP THE UNFOLDING OF POTENTIAL. IT IS THE MOST POWER-
FUL force on the planet. A tree root can lift a highway; species evolve against incredible
odds; and humans adapt to every challenge. The potential of life itself is estimated to be
so powerful that, even if we destroyed all life on the planet, it would emerge again in another
form. It is estimated that the potential field has enough energy stored within a cubic centimeter
of empty space to recreate the entire universe. Civilizations may rise and fall but the potential
field will always manifest itself anew. Who can doubt that we should study the unfolding of potential?

In all its variations of form, the potential field has a built in order. All life grows according to this order. Even a stream of supposedly random numbers, generated on a computer,
takes on magnificent fractal forms. These forms are as beautiful as anything visible to us as a
human race and they are enfolded within randomness.

Since everything is made of information in motion, the entire species of humankind is
part of the manifestation of the information emanating from a field of potential. All consciousness in held in place, takes its form, and manifests itself as part of the quantum potential field.
This explanation provides a framework that is inclusive. It embraces all that is know and presents a context that provides deep meaning in what we are experiencing. It also works. It becomes possible to find solutions to every problem we face and for the integration of every
school of thought and every science for everything that is known at the present time.

Information is the fabric of the whole dynamic. The study of its diverse and varied
manifestations we have come to refer to as the study of Holodynamics. As conscious beings we
can attune ourselves to this all-encompassing information field. We have found that we, each of
us who is here, have made it possible, even easy, to align with our own personal Full Potential
Self and then to unfold our life potential both individually and collectively.

This alignment opens the source of life energy and allows us to manifest a passion for
life in a most powerful way. There is nothing more satisfying, nothing more rewarding and
nothing more important than unfolding our life potential. The unfolding process reveals the
meaning of life, the purpose of each person's path and unfolds the multiplicity of worlds in
which we live.

Empowering potential is the activity of an aligned person, the state of being one with
the universe and the demonstration of a master of life. It is the state of being Holodynamic.

There is no better course to take in life than to follow the unfolding of potential. It begins with the exploration of one's own potential. It begins with the personal experience of discovering one's Full Potential Self and learning to align with this potential so as to consciously help it unfold.

Assignment 29: Prepare a five minute introduction on Unfolding Potential. Be prepared to give this presentation without referring to your notes. Discuss with your Holon. Give the speech to a group.

Taking this course is personal. It is yours. There is no other potential like yours. Like your fingerprint, lip print, retina or brain waves, your Full Potential Self is unique to you. Aligning your conscious intention to its unfolding is to align with life. You soon realize that life is a process of self-discovery and self-fulfillment. Life is about unfolding potential.

Self-discovery is ultimately the discovery of your own potential self. It is the discovery of that potential field that drives you to greater and greater heights - to manifest your talents, your character and your loving nature when there is no earthly reason you would love the people you consider to be your enemies. Self-discovery is woven into the power that generates every situation in which you find yourself in life. It is part of the Covenant.

Taking the course of your Full Potential Self leads to deep and genuine self-confidence, self-assertion and amazing creativity. Creativity extends into the entire information field. Creativity makes a difference in the world and leaves your own unique *fingerprint* on the emergence of life potential.

The exercises that follow have been developed from a *"what-works"* approach in helping participants discover their potential (real) self. After all, if your Full Potential Self is driving the car, you may as well get in touch with the driver so you can discuss where you are going in life. These manuals work together in both helping master this information and teach it to others. These principles and processes accelerate the unfolding of potential, and the best thing about this information is that, when you apply them, these principles and processes work.

Becoming an Advocate is the first step in the Circles of Success series through which people master the subject matter and skills of reaching and maintaining that state of being Holodynamic. I spent decades of my life testing the possibility that complex problems could be solved. What I discovered is that they can be solved. This is about how you can learn to solve any problem, no matter how difficult it may seem.

In this outline, we follow the stages of the implicate order by which potential in unfolded. This course, for example, has seven sections that follow an implicate order: **section one** is focused upon how to empower the unfolding of personal potential; **section two** shows how to align your holodynes with your Full Potential Self through tracking; **section three** deals with overcoming blocks to our emerging potential (through tracking); **section four** deals with teaming up to unfold potential in the community and in the world of work; **section five** deals with *becoming aligned* with the potential of the planet; **section six** focuses upon extending one's own potential into that state of being a planetary Potentializer; and **section seven** helps prepare those who want to share and teach this information.

Assignment 30: Review the entire course outline on Unfolding Potential. Discuss with your Holon the context for each section and then how the content for each is coherent. Make notes.

Most of us are but faintly aware of the potential that is emerging. Most people have almost no understanding of the quantum potential field, the nature of the implicate order, the mechanisms through which consciousness manifests and influences life, nor of how it all applies in their lives. This lack of knowing puts us at a handicap and, at the same time, presents us with an opportunity.

The world around us is going through exponential growth. We have moved from wandering, gathering nomads to agricultural city-states from which civilization emerged with its pyramids of power and feudal systems. Next we came through an Industrial Revolution that spawned the great monolithic nationhoods that divided up the world into superpowers. The power struggles between nations brought on cataclysmic wars and, for almost a half a century, nations were ruled by a *Cold War* strategy, with its great walls and iron curtains.

Recently, these walls have been tumbling down as in the collapse of Communism in the Soviet Union and the fall of the Berlin Wall. We are all caught in the turmoil of the restructuring of these global interests. Power systems have evolved into international corporate interests, and terrorism is now "the enemy" of nations. These events are symptomatic of an even more remarkable phenomenon. More and more of the walls that separate people are beginning to dissolve. We are becoming collectively aware that separation is an illusion.

Information, power and economics are being democratized. Everyone has a chance to *play in the games* once reserved only for the rich and powerful. More and more people are realizing they can have a piece of the pie. Everyone can unfold their fullest potential. It is an age of individualization within a context of globalization.

Assignment 31: Consider each of these points and discuss them in your Holon. What does the future hold? How can one person or one group begin to understand and take part in a way that will make a constructive difference? How does our past help us understand what is happening now? How does consciousness emerge from one age to the next age; from nomad tribes to international entities? What is next? Where are we headed and can one person really make any difference at all?

The future holds the potential of a *collective leap* in consciousness. It all depends upon how aware we become about unfolding the potential of ourselves and the planet. Our next individual and global step is to understand how to empower the unfolding of potential.

HOW TO EMPOWER POTENTIAL

The Three Patterns of Potential:

Potential manifests in three fundamental patterns. It manifests as **particles**, as **waves** and as **presence**. For those who advocate a Holodynamic view of reality, unfolding potential requires a working knowledge of all three patterns.

The first section of this course has to do with the *particle* sciences, including physics, biology, holographics, information theory and developmental psychology.

The second section will deal with the *wave* dynamics and will focus on the processes and skill development that helps participants focusing on potential and manifesting it according to their own will.

It is third section that deals with the manifestation of presence that unfolds the greatest potential of all. There are no real solutions to anything in particle and wave dynamics. Real solutions emerge from presence. You must be *present* in order to make a real difference in this world.

The Six Steps of Potentializing:

In the Unfolding Potential Seminars, you will learn *the six steps of potentializing*. It is within potentializing that you will be exposed to some of the concepts, principles, findings and processes involved in the whole dynamic.

For detailed information, each of the manuals will unfold more and more depth regarding the teaching of Holodynamics. To begin, we focus on the process of Potentialization, or the unfolding of potential.

The unfolding of potential, or the process of potentialization, is a natural order. When physics is applied to developmental psychology, the implicate order shows up as stages of development. In life, this means that each person goes through natural, built-in stages of development.

The first step in this process is to focus on the potential desired. Once you are able to identify what you want, the mind is like a camera. You will basically get what you have focused upon. Here are the natural steps of the potentializing process:

• Align with your Full Potential Self.

• Then align the intimate team of like-minded people who are unfolding the same potential.

•Next, begin to build an organizational system that is dedicated to unfolding the potential together. This gives the potential an infrastructure.

•One must also align one's principles and maintain a state of coherence.

•This allows the team to extend outward into the world and manifest the desired potential.

Exercise 32: Discuss the distinctions that are possible when a person understands the three patterns through which potential manifests. How do these three patterns affect the six steps of potentialization? Make notes.

The process of potentialization is natural. It is done all the time. Still, it also fails many times. In America for example, it is estimated that 98 percent of all start-up companies fail. The process is not complicated, but people tend to have many blocks to this natural process. Therefore, we teach the three patterns and the six steps of potentialization, which also teaches how to identify and transform the hidden blocks so the road to success is clear and the way is easy.

1. FOCUS ON POTENTIAL

A. WHAT IS WANTED?

Ask people what they want. Write it on charts. Put it up in front of them for all to see. Discuss it. Wants reflect a hidden potential within that is pushing its way out. The "en-folded" potential can be "un-folded" through the focus of conscious intent. Our first job is to teach focus on the potential that is waiting to manifest in people's lives.

People know what they want most of the time. In other cases, they "think" they know or "feel" what they desire, but these thoughts and feelings are unclear reflections of a deeper potential waiting to unfold. Therefore, it helps to know certain concepts that help clear intent and align consciousness to the hidden potential.

B. THE CAMERA OF THE MIND

One way to look at potential is to view the mind as a camera. Information, coming into the mind, comes through the lenses of the senses. Our lenses are like the lens of the camera. The information is received through (fine-grained and gross-grained) screens that determine what the senses see, hear, taste, touch and smell, etc. Draw this out for people to see. Let them get the picture of information coming in through their senses.

The information is processed Holodynamically. That is, it is received through the fine-grained and gross-grained sensory lenses and "spun" into a holographic code (a Gaborian Transform) so it can be stored in the microtubules. (Don't worry if you don't understand all this right now. The manuals explain quite completely the basic biology and quantum mechanics of sensory processing. If you want more information on this, read *The Dance of Life* and refer also to authors such as Penrose and Hameroff, Hawking, Pribram, etc. in the references).

C. HOLODYNES

Information coming through the senses is transformed and stored as holodynes. Holodynes come in three distinctive types. They contain particle, wave and Holodynamic information (in-form-at-i-on).

PARTICLE holodynes serve rational and linear thinking.
WAVE holodynes serve as carriers for emotional dynamics.
PRESENCE holodynes provide the vehicle for states of being.

Information coming through the senses is *compressed* and made ready for instant recall. In its compressed state, information is subconscious. Still, it is potentially active. Like quantum computers, holodynes are *on* and *off* at the same time. For more on this subject, refer to *The Dance of Life* Chapter III.

Holodynes resonate according to certain frequencies (Frohlech's frequencies that are 10 to the minus 33 per second). It is believed these frequencies cause quantum coherence in the body, which gives the body an integritous movement and sense of being.

Holodynes become self-organizing and take on a life of their own. Thus, they emerge as self-conscious entities with *causal potency,* which means they have the power to cause things to happen. Holodynes run the body and control the mind. They also control disease, personality traits, relationships and every other type of dynamic in one's life.

Holodynes are like computer programs only much more advanced. Once formed, holodynes program your life. Holodynes are dynamic, so the good news is that they can change, transform and mature. It all depends upon the information they have at their disposal. You, the conscious being who is present, can guide your holodynes.

It can be hypothesized that short-term memory occurs when the holodynes are first transmitted into the water environment within the microtubules. Long-term memory occurs when the dimer molecules that make up the wall of the microtubules form valence patterns, which hold the information in place, giving stability to the holodynes. This turns into long-term memory when the dimers grow arms (MAPS) which hold the information frequencies in place. MAPS form at exactly the point where they stabilize the harmonics of each holodyne, thus giving memory long-term duration. (This would be a great experiment for someone interested in the biological mechanics of consciousness).

Assignment 33: Construct a half-hour presentation on the microtubules. Discuss the pertinent points you would make in giving this presentation to a group of medical doctors or professional psychologists. Make notes.

D. DECOMPRESSION

Each holodyne is a miniature information system. It has its own parameters, resonating frequencies and, for all intents and purposes, may be considered as a *compressed icon* like on a computer board. By focusing on the icon, you can *decompress* the information contained within the holodyne. By "icon" I mean an *event horizon* that contains the information that takes form as a holodyne.

A single event horizon may contain more than one holodyne or even an entire network of holodynes. It's like a country. The United States is made up of many different states, which are made up of many different networks of cities, which contain many people. Yet the United States is contained within one event horizon that has its own boundaries. The way to find out what is contained within your own event horizons, within your own mind, is simply to focus on a single holodyne. It will tell you all about the country in which it lives.

The first thing that happens is that the holodyne itself manifests. It can be consciously triggered. Skilled focus can be used to create a morphogenic field, or a growing environment, in which the potential of the information of the holodyne is invited to unfold. If you go to war against the holodyne, war will result. If you create a field of appreciation and exploration, growth results.

These *fields* are *growing environments* that, on a larger scale, create the circumstances of your life. So holodynes have their own event horizon. Groups of holodynes (such as personality traits, archetypes, even goals, a sense of purpose, beliefs and cultural rituals) can be held within an event horizon and carried by groups of people and these form the fabric of collective consciousness.

In their *particle* form, holodynes control the "f-stops" (as in a camera) and focus mechanisms of your mind. In this way, holodynes create *selective perception*.

Immature holodynes create immature perception, which controls the field and which is why people don't get what they want. In our journey into consciousness, we will unveil deeper and deeper levels of information about how these control mechanisms work.

Information organizes by three processes: linear, non-linear (quantum) and hyperspacial at the same time. This appears to be true everywhere in nature. The linear dynamics control rational thoughts and the logic of our thinking processes.

In their wave state, holodynes control feeling and emotions. They create selective energy fields that keep people endlessly involved in emotional games. People caught up in such games are not to manifest what they potentially might be able to manifest because they are so busy playing in the games.

There are usually no solutions to anything in a mind that is locked into particle and/or wave dynamics. Solutions come from the Holodynamic state of being present.

The *Holodynamic state of being present* potentially contains everything you want. In order to *collapse the wave* and manifest what you want, you must focus and take the cup of opportunity and dip it into the quantum potential field. This process begins by focusing upon what is wanted. You get what you focus on because it gives *form* to the potential field.

Assignment 34: Role-play a situation (any situation will do. If you need models, refer to Manual III). Stop the role-play and discuss how a specific holodyne has an event horizon in which it thrives. Discuss how such event horizons can be transformed along with the holodyne. Make notes.

E. YOUR SENSES

Each of your senses has mechanisms through which you focus attention. Some people are visually dominant. Their focus is mostly through their eyes. Others are auditory and their focus is mainly on what they hear. Others are kinesthetic and do a lot of touching in order to communicate. People can use an intuitive sense of energy, temperatures or smell. Most people use a mixture of senses and are quite eclectic about it.

When communicating, it is helpful if one's reference matches that of their partner. It's like speaking the same language. People understand you better when you speak the same language. People also get the meaning of your communication better when you use the same sensory perception process. If they have a dominant sense, speak in that language – use that sense. Here is an exercise that will help participants identify their dominant sense.

Assignment 35: Walk around the room (participants walk around the room). Ask: "What do you sense?" Then discusses which sense each person is using.

Sensory input can also be controlled by one's information processing system. If you are linear, you will experience your senses in a rational way. If your information management system is non-linear, you will be oriented to emotional dynamics while if you are in a certain state of being, all of your senses will register your situation in a different way.

For example, if you are rational, from a Newtonian/Cartesian view, the world is a linear, mechanical machine. Your senses are input mechanisms and that's all.

From a quantum perspective, senses are waves. They process information as if the information was a vehicle on a two-way street. What you focus upon is affected by your focus. What is focused on responds to the focus.

If you are aware of the whole dynamic, the world around you is a living, dynamic, interactive conscious field and you are the co-creator of the reality you are sensing. There are many scientific experiments that show this - especially at the micro level among the electrons and photons of the inner atom (see Appendix C and the Suggested Reading List in Appendix A).

One way to look at the impact of focus on the field of interactive, conscious potential is to view it as an *echo* effect. Focus creates an echo wave which, according to theorists, seem to go back and forward in time. I believe this happens within the liquid environment of the microtubules.

The quantum potential field, which is found at the center of the microtubules, provides the perfect mechanism for an information feedback system that connects directly to hyperspacial dimensions. This is one of the mechanisms of consciousness that indicate we are constantly interacting with parallel worlds.

The walls of the microtubules protect the delicate information exchange so it limits interference from other forms and fields of information. In this protected environment, your conscious network becomes sensitive to distinctions and provides you with your own unique information field. Event horizons can safely develop and become empowered.

The dimer switches provide the necessary valence patterns to hold our uniqueness in its place. The water molecules provide the multidimensional liquid medium for holographic memory storage. The single strings of water molecules that are directly connected to the quantum field are sufficient to carry both information and energy back and forth between this world and other worlds. Thus the boundary conditions are met for the interchange between worlds and to collapse the wave and create *us*. These mechanisms help set the stage for our causality. We can influence what we focus upon. We become co-creative.

Assignment 36: How does co-creation occur? What makes us capable of connecting to others? How is it that we experience collective intent? Discuss.

One central element is that holodynes are the carriers of information through valenced biological systems and quantum resonating frequencies. These information mechanisms, when combined with the implicate order, become self-organizing, living information systems. They are holographic in nature and are activated by conscious focus. When we change our focus, we access the holodynes. When we change the holodynes, we change our view of reality. Our gross-grained and fine-grained screens *shift*.

When people walk around a room just sensing the room and each other, you can tell by their conscious focus which senses are dominant.

Assignment 36 continued: Ask participants: Do they hear the sounds around them? Do they smell the scents in the room? Do they recognize the Full Potential Self of other people? Where is their focus? Are they particle, wave or Holodynamic in their focus?

This information provides tools by which we can communicate better and support our co-creative activities within a harmonic that is comfortable to others. This is helpful when you are tracking someone or listening to a holodyne or learning to love another person. It is valuable for teaming up, teaching or extending oneself into the universe.

Assignment 37: Divide the room into two sections.

Explain that the people on one side of the room are to be totally rational while the people on the other side are totally emotional.

Ask the group to present a question.

Have each side of the room answer the question from their (rational or emotional) perspective.

Create a situation among a representative from each side of the room (any situation will do). Have participants observe and comment.

Do the same for one of the senses.

Observe how differently participants who are using different senses experience the room and the situational dynamics of any set of circumstances.

Awareness of sensory dynamics is one dimension of a multidimensional field. In order to grasp how various dynamics work together to produce this particular set of circumstances call life, it helps to have a model of consciousness. Using the model helps one better understand the whole dynamic of life.

F. THE MIND MODEL

In order to help keep all this straight, I created a topological model of consciousness. This came to be known as *the Mind Model.* The topological Mind Model represents a general picture of the dynamics involved in consciousness. It helps to demonstrate how classical particle dynamics, quantum wave dynamics and presence combine with holodynes, family and cultural field dynamics.

This combination produces an echo effect that, when it meets the boundary conditions, *collapses the potential wave,* and *creates a manifest reality.* This is why the mind model is placed at the center of the potentializing process.

Our senses act as *funnels* through which the information is organized and correlated with relative information from parallel hyperspacial dimensions.

Each sense has screens that act as *form-givers* so that information is received in a specific form. Therefore, when we focus on the senses, *the gatekeepers of our holodynes* become active.

The *gatekeeper holodynes* are control programs. They are part of a magnificent and elaborate implicate order coming from parallel worlds of the past, present and future. All are contained and maintained with that *state of being* that is outside the limitations of space and time. They are part of the domain of the Full Potential Self. To better understand the whole dynamic, you must understand the function of the gatekeepers and how to get beyond their control.

The Mind Model can help you get beyond your gatekeepers. It is like an icon that reminds us of the whole dynamic of life in one picture (See Appendix A). When you are held in one position (as in a static belief system or a social more', etc.), you can step beyond that static position by referring to the Mind Model and sensing where you are and what your next step is on the path to emerging your fullest possible potential.

Assignment 38: Study the Mind Model. Form into groups of six. Discuss each dimension represented in the model. For example, you may want to discuss how does each dimension of the mind model affect your personal, social and/or professional life?

G. SENSITIVITY

You can become more sensitive to your senses by exploring which senses are dominant. This can be done in a seminar by asking: *"What senses are you using?"*

Assignment 39: Ask class participants to walk around the room with their eyes closed. Cutting out one sense amplifies others and often raises abnormal fears from people who are visually dominant. Ask them to share. Then, ask them to plug their ears as they walk around the room. What did they sense when one or more of their senses are blocked?

How many senses are there? There are estimated to be more than 384 specific senses within the body. A sense of balance, direction, migration, thirst, hunger, elimination, danger and many others are fairly easy for most people to recognize. On a more subtle level, thought and emotion may also be senses, along with ambition and drive. In other words, holodynes also have senses but, in order to be aware of such senses, one must be aware of holodynes.

It's a trick question but there are so many senses that you would hardly notice one that is most common. "Do you have common sense?"

Assignment 40: Discuss common sense. How does common sense relate to collective consciousness?

People often ask: "What is the sixth sense?" Your *sixth* sense is that sense which is beyond the reach of your normal five senses of touch, taste, smell, hearing and sight. It is usually thought of as a sense of subtle energy through which the body serves as an antenna system, taking in information and putting it through the limbic center (see Rosin and Becker).

This subtle energy sense emanates from the Full Potential Self as part of the information system transceived through Frohlech's frequencies.

The choices we make depend upon the dimension of consciousness we are using.

"Energy," for example, is a wave dynamic.

"Potential" is a dimension of presence.

Each is a different state of being and, while both involve choice, the frame of mind being used may result in different views of reality and different results.

This sense of subtle energies is a wave dynamic. It is part of the whole dynamic. This sense works according to the holographic principle of *"What is known to the part is known to the whole and what is known to the whole is known to the part."*

The holographic dimension becomes more obvious when we look at works such as those of researcher Cleave Baxter. Cleave uses polygraphs on plants. He found that plants are conscious and are very sensitive to what is going on around them. His work with two palm trees showed that the palm trees were conscious of who was present in the room. His work also included cell response to host conditions. He found that there exists a direct frequency communication through subtle energy senses between the conscious self and all parts of the body even when separated by long distances.

Within this system of thought, the limbic center is seen as central to controlling each person's *hypothalamic*/pituitary/hormonal systems through quantum frequencies. This system is considered to be made up of *altered states of consciousness*. In other words, plants have holodynes. It is part of the bioenergetics system and its relationship to the quantum wave is managed through holodynes by the hyperspacial counterpart of each plant. All living things seem to have a Full Potential Self.

Energy is not enough of a framework to explain our senses. All input through the senses is triadic. It comes as particle and wave. It also had a dimension of presence. Energy is *Holodynamic*.

The retina of the eye contains the periphery (wave sensitive) and the fovea (particle sensitive) that feed their intake information into the optical nerve which transforms the information holographically, processes it through the right and left brain regions for intuitive and ra-

75

tional processing.

The ear contains the eardrum (wave sensitive) and the coiled colloquia (particle sensitive) which do the same. All senses reflect this triadic nature. All systems have ionic spinners that take the information, integrate it and *spin* it (a Gaborian transforming process) so it can be stored in Holodynamic form within the microtubules where it comes alive. It becomes part of your mind.

Intuitive Sensory Perception (ISP) is also the process by which the mind handles information input. ISP is an under-utilized capacity, which allows every individual to discover orders within orders of power and potential within their mind. It allows a direct, specific process by which holodynes can be accessed, tracked and matured. ISP offers creative intuitive processes for potentializing your life. It is a triadic process. ISP is correlated to the way information processes in rational, emotional and creative systems.

Training in Holodynamics attempts to demonstrate how all things work together harmonically. We begin with focus, the senses, how holodynes are formed, how they respond back into the field and control focus. The exploration of our senses, including ISP, can help create what is wanted. We honor both particle and wave dynamics as part of a holographic effect that comes alive as self-organizing information systems. Once we understand the Holodynamic of nature and of life, we are able to see the potential within any given set of circumstances.

Assignment 41: Sit face-to-face with a partner. Using ISP, tune into the Full Potential Self of your partner. Write down what you sense and then share it with your partner. In what ways does your ISP agree with your partner's sense of their Full Potential Self? Do you disagree on anything? Make notes.

ISP works well in life. It allows for individual and collective thought and for creative choice. The first choice is to choose what to focus upon. So we ask: "What do you want?"

2. ALIGNING WITH THE FULL POTENTIAL SELF

The single most powerful process on the planet is to align with your Full Potential Self. The Full Potential Self is the source of your personal power. It contains information from all dimensions of reality, including that from parallel worlds, and gives you access to the past and the future.

Once aligned with your Full Potential Self, it is possible to reach into the past and transform any information field. From this state of being it is possible to shift your family tree and even impact cultural fields. It is also possible to reach into the future and bring it into the present. It is when you are aligned with your Full Potential Self that your are truly *present*.

Being *present* represents living life to its fullest possible potential and holding both the past and the present in a loving embrace. The state of being *one* with the past and future creates a quantum coherence that supersedes both time and space.

The process for aligning with your Full Potential Self is simple and natural.

Assignment 42: Using your Intuitive Sensory Perception, imagine a Place of Peace. There, within the Place of Peace you are free to invite your Full Potential Self to take form, communicate and meet with you on a regular basis. To make this easy you can imagine a "round table" where you can sit together and discuss issues of the day. There, at the round table, you have direct access to any internal guides you choose. You can also access any holodynes you may want to deal with and this can all be done under the guidance of your Full Potential Self.

A. CREATING A PLACE OF PEACE

When you have a Place of Peace you can create peace at any time by triggering the memory of your Place of Peace. Such recall sets up a morphogenic field of peace throughout your body and mind. Whatever you do, will tend to come from peace. Peace is a state of quantum coherence that is aligned with your fullest potential.

Assignment 43: Imagine a Place of Peace. Using all of your senses, see, smell, touch, taste (if possible) and feel it. Take upon yourself a state of being peace. Draw out on a piece of paper your Place of Peace.

Having a Place of Peace can be a great comfort when you want step beyond any situation. Suppose, for example, you are driving on the freeway and someone cuts in front of you causing you to slam on the breaks. Instead of going into some form of road rage cussing them out, honking your horn or driving wildly after them in some erratic manner, you can choose to go to your Place of Peace, observe the dynamics and choose how to act to unfold the potential of that situation.

Your Place of Peace resonates with a frequency of peace from which you can establish new patterns beyond war and beyond old holodynes that have been controlling your behavior and provides a base camp from which you can negotiate for effective living from a state of being present.

Assignment 44: For the next week, keep track of the times when you are confronted with emotional upheaval. Each time this happens, consciously go to your Place of Peace instead of reacting. Keep a record and share your results.

B. ACCESSING YOUR FULL POTENTIAL SELF

Once at peace, you are more open to the consequences that <u>unfold</u> more of the <u>enfolded</u> potential that you have within you. To choose peace is to choose life. The more you resonate with such choices, the more of your life potential will open to you. The ultimate life potential you have is contained within your Full Potential Self.

Assignment 45: Use your senses to intuitively perceive your Full Potential Self. Imagine, coming toward you in your Place of Peace, you at your fullest potential. Use your senses to see, smell, touch and experience your Fullest Potential Self. Can you sense what qualities your FPS has? Can you communicate with your FPS? Does your FPS have any messages for you? Write down your experience including the qualities you sense and any messages from your FPS. What does your FPS look like? What qualities does your FPS manifest to you? What messages does your FPS have for you?

This is a natural process. Your Full Potential Self exists in hyperspace. You can access this dimension of your own personal reality, anytime. When would *now* be the best time?

C. SUSTAINING A MORPHOGENIC FIELD

A morphogenic field is a growing environment in which your fullest potential can emerge. It produces a Full Potential Self *effect* in personal living. You can use your Full Potential Self to help you decide what you want, to guide you in life, to help you potentialize projects and to help you access *holodynes* and mature them.

Assignment 46: Identify a specific issue that blocks success. Write down the issue at hand.

Continue the meditation process in which participants imagine a communication with their FPS. Ask your full potential self to serve as you personal "knower": Explain that they can access the part of their mind that "knows" by tuning in to their Full Potential Self and developing a personal relationship. Ask the FPS to share an understanding on the issue at hand. Were they able to get a sense of the answer? Did the communication aid in achieving more success? Discuss.

Your Full Potential Self can be a conscious doorway into the dimensions of your mind that contains intuitive knowing and the Holodynamic dimensions of reality.

D. ACCESSING THE FULL POTENTIAL SELF OF OTHER PEOPLE

Your Full Potential Self can guide you in relating, solving problems and creating deep bonding and intimacy. It can give you information about others through their FPS.

By *tuning in to* your Full Potential Self you open yourself to information from the intuitive hyperspacial dimensions of your life. You become a walking antenna. Your mind extends beyond your body. You begin to access the resonating energy fields that emanate from all life. You become aware of quantum field dynamics and energy frequencies, the information they contain and you grow in your ability to sense the causal potency within holodynes.

Assignment 47: Stand face-to-face, with a partner. Go to your Place of Peace. Call upon your Full Potential Self and ask permission to call forth the Full Potential Self of your partner. What do you sense?

Do they know each other? Cam you sense what is going on between your Full Potential Self and your partner's Full Potential Self? Discuss with your partner the experience of sharing FPS to FPS.

3. ALIGNING WITH HOLODYNES

Life becomes more fun. We sense the celebration of all life and the lessons to be learned even from downdraft dynamics – especially from downdraft dynamics! We sense the path. We fear nothing because everything is part of the whole dynamic. There are lessons to learn and choices to make.

Everything becomes part of the natural order by which holodynes grow and our part is clear. We can help accelerate that growth. It is in our nature to do so. It is part of the love we are. We are each part of the celebration of life.

Assignment 48: Go back through the events of your life. Choose an event that you believe was a very downdraft event. How did you experience that event? What, if anything, stops you from celebrating the event? What, if anything, would you like to do about it?

A. HOLODYNES ARE ENTITIES

Holodynes have personality. They can cause things to happen in your daily life in some very personal ways. Holodynes can program your thoughts, emotions and your experiences. They are a key programming center for what you see, hear, taste, touch and think ahead.

To potentialize your life, you must learn to relate to your holodynes. You will naturally seek some way to relate your inner friends. Just as you seek relationships with the people around you, you will seek relationships with your holodynes.

Within these relationships you will discover that you have the power to potentialize your holodynes. This process of potentializing your holodynes is part of the process of potentializing yourself. In fact, most of the time you must align your relationship with your holodynes *first* before you can make any real difference in your own level of enlightenment.

This can be done by inviting our holodynes into our Place of Peace and arranging for a conflict resolution process to begin.

Assignment 49: How good a friend are you to yourself? Inside, are you the type of friend that you would like to hang out with, spend time, discuss things and know with confidence that you are a real friend? Write your thoughts and discuss them with your support group.

B. TRACKING HOLODYNES

Tracking sets up alignment between yourself and the fullest potential of your holodynes. It provides greater conscious awareness and control over the realms of your subconscious. This is one of the most important steps in solving the complex problems of the world. Tracking is an ISP process. You can use your intuitive dimension of reality to access, befriend, and transform holodynes.

In this process you are able to bond Full-Potential-Self to Full-Potential-Self with your holodynes. You set up an internal system, beginning at your Place of Peace, you can gather your holodynes around your Round Table and relate openly and honestly with each holodyne.

You can communicate regularly on a daily basis. This process changes the information and thus the physics of our mind. It allows old energy patterns to change.

New morphogenic fields are created. New event horizons emerge. You can create your own version of quantum coherence, one that allows more consciousness and a clearer channel for your personal power to manifest what you want.

Tracking is a natural process for holodynes. Holodynes love it. It has a positive impact upon you as well. You will love the effects. Everybody wins. It is consciously taking holodynes through the natural order of their own growth. You potentialize your holodynes.

Tracking is an internal *reach*. It takes you into your family and cultural beliefs as well and helps mature those holodynes that have been passed on to you through your family and cultural belief systems for generations.

Assignment 50: Track your holodynes. Pair off and sit facing each other. Have one person be the tracking facilitator and the other be the participant who is being tracked.

For those not familiar with the tracking process, provide the tracking guide (in appendix E) and demonstrate how it is used by tracking a volunteer in front of the group.

Once everyone is familiar with the tracking process, have participants identify an issue and, with the aid of a facilitator, access the holodynes orchestrating the issue and track them.

Once the tracking is completed, switch roles. The participant becomes the facilitator and tracks the one who was the facilitator.

Part of the job of a Facilitator is to keep notes so that, when the process is done, the one being tracked has a record of the entire event.

C. MANAGING CHAOS

People fear chaos but it is a normal part of change. Any new development requires re-organization, an emergence from one event horizon to the next. Changes in the way we process information create normal chaos.

Even tracking can create chaos. In order to better prepare participants for handling chaos, we suggest there are four ways to approach chaos.

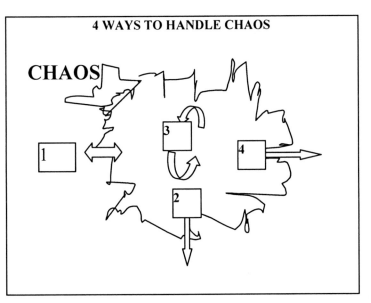

4 WAYS TO HANDLE CHAOS

CHAOS

1. Avoid chaos

2. Substitute potential for a lesser choice

3. Endlessly cycle in the chaos

4. Stay focused on potential to be unfolded

Assignment 51: Discuss: Under what conditions in your life do you tend to use one of these alternatives to chaos?

The key to overcoming the effects of chaos is to understand the *potential* within the field of chaos. There is really no such thing as chaos - just as there is no such thing as randomness. There is no disorder anywhere in the universe. What we think of as chaos really turns out to be something we don't yet understand.

Every circumstance in which we believe there is chaos has been proven to contain a hidden order. When we create a random number distribution system, it turns out that the numbers are not random at all. All such number generators project a hidden order (fractals). Fractals show orders within orders of profound beauty that were not evident before we learned how to see them.

Likewise, there are also such hidden orders within orders of the human mind. William James, one of the father's of modern psychology once told the story of a woman who came up to him after one of his lectures and said, "Dr. James. This world is flat and it sits upon the back of a great turtle. What do you think of that?" He smiled and responded, "Why its very simple, madam. It's turtles all the way down!"

There are hidden influences, *subtle attractors*, enfolded within the streams of thought in our mind. Subtle attractors reflect hidden orders within gravitational fields. These are called *Lorenz Attractors* in physics and can be seen in such things as the swing of a pendulum or the motion of air. There are many subtle attractors that are unseen, but still in effect, within the fields of consciousness.

In truth, science knows very little about the subtle attractors of consciousness. We have barely uncovered the effect of quantum dynamics, resonating frequencies, hyperspacial dynamics, or the effects of information fields and holodynes on our perception of reality. How much effect does the cosmos, for example, have on our state of consciousness?

D. YOUR MIND and INFINITY

It is interesting to look at a Kotch curve and actually see a demonstration of how *infinity* can be drawn *within* a given space. Perhaps the mind has a similar ability. Could the Holodynamic part of the mind comprehend infinity? Our experience gives a clear answer. It can and it does, but you can only become aware of this from a Holodynamic state of being.

TO CREATE A
KOTCH CURVE

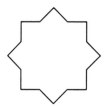

KEEP ON ADDING TRIANGLES
ALONG THE EDGES. HOW MANY
CAN YOU ADD?

Assignment 52: Discuss in your small group: Do you have any evidence that your consciousness contains an awareness of infinity or anything beyond confinements of time and space?

E. YOUR MIND and PERMANENT CHAOS

We can show how Jupiter, the planet, has a *permanent storm* that is referred to as *the eye of* Jupiter. At the center is a strange shape which, when put into the computer for simulation turns out to be a *fractal*. It is possible to create an exact simulation of same proportions to the eye of Jupiter. In reality, the permanent chaotic storm of Jupiter may be an extended fractal.

The human mind can also produce permanent chaos. Information fields can cycle in the mind, as if it is locked into a form of continual chaos. Anger, fear, hate and other forms of mental/emotional chaos become contained within their own event horizons. For all intents and purposes, they are considered as *permanent* chaos in the human mind. This situation can be changed.

Tracking puts new information into the cycling process and opens the event horizon to its fullest possible potential. This process is essential to create a new order of life. It is done by unfolding the potential within the chaos which unlocks the hidden potential and changes the way the information is manifesting in reality.

Assignment 53: Choose a pattern that seems to create permanent chaos in your life (or at least seems to trigger a continual response that has no apparent solution). Describe it in your journal. Discuss it with your Holon.

F. THE HOLOGRAPHICS OF HOLODYNES

There is a school of thought that deals with geometric designs. This school of thought has a great deal to say about the designs of nature and of consciousness (see Dan Winter for example). It is evident that within the water media of the microtubules, water molecules store and hold the memory of such geometric designs. These designs are part of the *in-form-ation* system at the heart of holodynes.

We know we can use our intuition to access holodynes and that, when we do, they mostly have shapes and colors. In fact, they seem to have correlative frequencies to every one of our senses. They have taken on form according to the information they contain.

The most interesting thing about holodynes is that they also are the carriers of information that reflects entire patterns of behavior. We suspect that each shape and color, sound or sense, is directly connected to a *form-u-la* or the *form you give it*.

It may also be associated with the flow of subtle attractors that make up the field of information from which it comes. In other words, a holodyne may be a type of fractal or a hidden order within orders.

Consciousness has shapes, colors, tones and other dynamics within its information systems that are intricately interwoven into its pattern and flow of perception, memory and power to manifest. After all, our senses are continually feeding into the entire field of consciousness. Information is also being continually fed into the system from hyperspace. This information is all contained within the holodynes. In some ways, the exact information depends upon the *source* of the information.

Holodynes have four major sources at the foundation of their existence.

- First, holodynes are inherited. They come down through the microtubules of the sperm and egg. It's a biological fact. We inherit everything from our parents. Potentially we inherit the entire pool of information coming from our ancestors.

- Second, we have our holodynes modeled by our family and culture. We learn by association and the most primal of all our associations are those received early in our childhood. There we get our first impressions of life, its meaning and all its games.

- Third, we make up our own holodynes. We are creative, have active imaginations and we can decide how life is and our mind forms holodynes that reflect our imagined reality.

- Fourth, we are constantly receiving information from hyperspacial dimensions. This information comes from parallel worlds where our Full Potential Self has many other expressions of its potential and is constantly sharing these experiences. This is where many gifts, talents and intuitive genius insights originate.

These varied and intermingling sources make us very unique and give us each a different view of life.

Assignment 54: Getting from "a" to "be": Have the participants in the group number of one, two, one, two until everyone has a number.

Have those with the number one form a line in the center of the room (move all chairs to make room). Have those with the number two forms another line facing those with number one. Have the lines separate so they form a football shape.

Explain that the number ones become a team pitted against the numbers two team. Have team one applaud the game as the facilitator raises his arm to demonstrate the ability of team one to applaud. Do the same for team two. The "winning team" gets to go first.

Mark point "a" at one end of the football (line) and mark point "be" at the other end. Point "a" represent where we are and point "be" represents where we want to get to when we unfold potential.

Have the winning team proceed from point "a" to "be" one at a time with instructions that they must do it in an entirely unique way. In other words no person can do it the same as any other person. The punishment is that they will have to go back and do it all over again. Everyone encourages participants as they do this exercise.

At the end of the first team's effort, the facilitator checks with the other team to make sure that no one copied anyone else's efforts.

The facilitator then instructs the second team to get from point "a" to "be" without duplicating anyone else's actions. Everyone encourages them and, as the last person completes the assignment the facilitator checks with the other team to make sure no one copied the others.

Facilitator then asks what participants learned from this experience. Was it fun?

Did anyone copy? Could anyone have copied "exactly"?

The point is that everyone has their own way of doing things. Each of us may even share the same purpose. It is the same with one's holodynes. Each holodyne has its own unique way of doing things. No two can be alike. Each has its own intention and many intentions are shared with other holodynes.

G. USING YOUR FULL POTENTIAL SELF AS YOUR GUIDE

Using the Full Potential Self as an internal, personal guide, it is possible to track the holodynes which are controlling patterns so that we can take conscious control of our lives and freely design our destiny together. The FPS becomes the central reference for your reality. The result is that you will unfold your potential to its fullest.

Assignment 55: For 30 days, consciously begin each day with a round-table session with your Full Potential Self. Ask: What is it you want me to do this day that can unfold my potential to its greatest potential?

Write down all instructions from your Full Potential Self. Follow them as faithfully as you would an appointment or instruction from a teacher.

Share with others your progress.

H. TRANSFORMING FAMILY HOLODYNES

Family holodynes are some of the most powerful holodynes on earth. They are inherited genetically. They are modeled almost exclusively for the first part of everyone's life. They are reinforced for the rest of our lives by family and cultural exposure and support.

They also harbor some of the most persistent dysfunctional holodynes which block potential. We inherit and have modeled some very strange holodynes.

Assignment 56: Sit facing a partner. Choose Partner A and Partner B:

The Facilitator says: "Partner A begins by saying 'My mother believed about some subject...' and Partner B will listen without interruption. We will assign you certain subjects to begin. Then you may assign your own subjects. After Partner A has completed a subject, switch, and Partner B will share the same saying. This exercise continues through each member of the family.

"My mother believed about ... (work, money, sex, or whatever).

"My father believed about ... (the same subject) and
"I believe about ... (the subject), etc.

Person B facilitates by listening without interruption. After each subject, switch partners.

As each person begins to understand the nature of their family holodynes, these understanding can be enhanced by doing role-plays, group sharing and partnering. The environment becomes one of fun. The joy of discovery ripples through the group as each member creates a field of support and discovery. Then holodynes, no matter how strange, are explored and tracked.

The entire procedure is used to step beyond and view our holodynes in an open arena. You can use the Mind Model to help keep things straight. Such open exchange, using a format that provides new, accurate information stimulates growth and systematic transformation of family holodynes. The same holds true for cultural holodynes.

I. TRANSFORMING CULTURAL HOLODYNES

Cultural holodynes - gleaned from school, church, peer groups and other social institutions - also control our lives. This does not mean such holodynes are *bad* or *good*. They just *are*. As Townsend suggests, all *p-branes* are created equal.

In order to align a holodyne with its potential, you must understand not only the holodyne involved, but you must recognize that each information system is both *in and out, off and on*, at the same time. They are in and out of their own potential. They are in and out of alignment. Stepping beyond their event horizons allows you a definite strategic advantage.

When you can sense a cultural belief system that limits your potential you can reach in and access and transform the holodynes within that event horizon. This includes working beyond your own unique set of holodynes. It may require dipping the cup of your own initiative into a larger pool of information. It is sometimes necessary because the field of others may be limiting your own field, limiting your thinking and thus curtailing your potential.

How can you possibly explore such dynamics? There is a whole tool box waiting for you. Role playing, for example, allows the exploration of such holodynes and, when the processes of Holodynamics are applied to the situational dynamics, cultural holodynes can be transformed.

Assignment 57: Role-play a situation in which culture seems to limit your (or others) unfolding potential. During a role-play, the facilitator can stop the interaction at any time and step-beyond to discuss the dynamics with the participants and with the group (refer to Manual III for role-play examples).

The change necessary to potentialize relationships occurs because we relate first within ourselves, among our holodynes. Holodynes *grow up* during this exchange and are so transformed within us that we mature our ability to relate to one another. The synergy within, among our holodynes, is so great that it creates an external *synergy* in our ability to relate to others. The internal synergy *precedes* our ability to form a synergistic relationship with someone else.

J. CREATING INTIMACY WITH HOLODYNES

When you track a holodyne, it becomes mature. It reaches its fullest potential. Once a holodyne is mature, you can consciously, with integrity, relate to it. You become friends. You build trust. Your mind becomes coherent and more empowered. You develop intimacy between yourself and your holodynes. Why? Because you are now aligned with the holodyne's Full Potential Self and your own Full Potential Self. You relate at the deepest level of unfolding potential. This is genuine intimacy. Such intimacy is pre-conditional to creating the process of intimacy among your friends.

Assignment 58: Discuss: Can you love another person more than you love yourself? Can you love yourself any more than you love your holodynes?

Intimacy among your holodynes produces intimacy in your relationship with family members. You become aware of the holodynes that control relationships. You become aware of the Being of Togetherness (BOT). The Being of Togetherness is a holodyne especially designed to handle relationship dynamics. Like any other holodyne, the BOT must be nurtured and nurtured. The BOT is a living being. Genuine intimacy emerges when the BOT is cultivated and holodynes and people are dealt with on a FPS TO FPS basis.

Assignment 59: Reflect upon a person you like least in the world. From your Place of Peace and in the presence of your FPS, invite that person at their fullest potential, to visit with you.

Imagine a conversation in which you discuss the real intent of that person in all the actions that occurred and caused you to like that person the least.

What unveils itself?

Does your Full Potential Self have any suggestions for you?

Does the FPS of the other person have any suggestions for you? What are those suggestions? List them.

Share with your partner. Will you follow the suggestions? When would now be a good time?

Nurturing the BOT creates intimacy deeper and deeper. Relationships potentialize. We model such dynamics in the course through our example and our role playing sessions. More details are given on the BOT and how to achieve intimacy in Manual III.

CHAPTER SIX

TEAMING UP

GENUINE TEAMWORK IS THE ESSENCE OF BUSINESS. BUSINESS BECOMES EASY AND effective when each person's holodynes are mature and able to work in coherence and integrity to accomplish set goals and tasks.

Teamwork begins within the mind. Team members work under the guidance of their Full Potentials. Their holodynes are all on the team. This approach was revolutionary to Boeing when their demands for product outstripped their ability to perform. It was people like Peggy Gilmore, who teamed up with other trainers in Boeing and produced a Holodynamic program, that turned the runaway chaos into a new era of cooperation at Boeing. Within two years, the company - once described by top executives, as *unmanageable* and possibly *too big to survive* - was able to get back on production schedule.

Your world of externals is governed by your internal world. How you perceive life, your job, your company and your contribution is governed by your internal *Board of Directors*. The holodynes of your internal world cooperate according to patterns that reflect themselves outward in the way you treat others around you. It is a smaller internal fractal that recreates itself in your outside world in a bigger way. When you gain conscious access to your internal holodynes that govern your life, you gain access to control of your external world as well.

This internal access and control can be accomplished through the use of your guides at your Round Table.

Why a *round* table? Because, in negotiations, humankind has evolved to the point where teams no longer require a table where someone sits *at the head* of the table. Position no longer determines power.

As you mature you become aware of the potential within others. You can invite each person into a working relationship. The same is true of your holodynes. As you invite your holodynes to meet with you and your Full Potential Self, you soon realize you can do the same with everyone around you. They become your team mates on an equal basis.

Others are valued participants. Each has a position of value and gifts to contribute. The entire system is represented. You can meet anytime around your private round table to conduct the daily business of running your person life and extending oneself into the team. Regular, organized meetings can be held, plans developed and action taken. The synergy comes from within every participant.

It is like joining a group of musicians. There are many types of musical groups. They vary from "rock" and "jazz" bands to marching bands and "old time favorites." Some musical groups form into complete symphony orchestras made of hundreds of highly accomplished musicians, all playing under the exact instructions of one director, all following exactly the same score. The music finds its way through these various combinations of musicians and touches our souls.

Assignment 60: Reflect: What type of music do you appreciate most?

Evaluate: What type of organization is usually involved in producing the music?

Discuss: What are the similarities between the organization of the music you like and the working of your own mind and the orchestration of your own lifestyle?

Whether it's a football team, a business team or a musical group, participants team up to produce results according to their internal programming. The results they achieve are based upon inherent talent, skill levels, practice and dedication. Their bodies become instruments dedicated to the manifestation of an internal state of being.

A. COMMITMENT AND THE TEAM FOCUS

Team members are required to commit to following through with the manifestation of the team's potential. Commitment is essential to success. But the extent to which people are able to commit is directly parallel to the degree they are committed to their internal world. How can people commit to something outside of themselves any stronger or any different than to the degree they are committed to themselves or to their holodynes?.

Commitment begins at home, inside yourself, at your Round Table. It begins in the nature of your personal commitment to your Full Potential Self. It follows through with a commitment to your intuitive guides and holodynes that you have tracked and promised to follow in your daily affairs.

Success is enhanced by a well-balanced approach. This includes taking care of your rational mind and your heart. Yes, you can have a great time mixing in with the holodynes that are part of your life. Yes, you can have a BOT that helps guide you in your most intimate relationships. Yes, even your friends and family can be at your Round Table and can be an integral part of the celebration of life.

It also helps to have the instructions from your guides placed in a personal daily planner. You list instructions from your guides and schedule in the times when you will follow through and implement their plan. In this way a balance between rational, intuitive and Holodynamic states of being are integrated into daily action plans. With all of this, it is wisdom to remember there is an implicate order to growth.

Assignment 61: Identify at least one team to which you are committed. Explore the causes of your commitment. Make notes in your journal.

B. STAGES OF DEVELOPMENT IN TEAMS

The Six Stages of Development are reflected in the Stages of Development Chart. This chart becomes a guide that keeps action aligned with potential. The Chart is a useful and fairly comprehensive outline that integrates developmental theory with team building.

Beginning at choice, in the middle of the chart, consciousness emerges upward or downward in step-by-step processes. If one folds the chart in half along the choice line, the downdraft dynamics are brought to solution by the updraft dynamics. The updraft reflects the positive potential of the downdraft dynamics.

The chart progresses from left to right as is reflected in the implicate order by which consciousness emerges. In the manuals that follow, detailed instructions will be given regarding the step by step process of using the chart as a guide for team building.

This information has been expanded for businesses. We designed a *Bird's Eye View* chart that shows the successive development of the infrastructure for building the necessary business structure in which a team can effectively function.

Assignment 62: Review the "bird's-eye view" chart and discuss how it can be applied in creating a new business.

C. USING THE MIND MODEL IN THE WORLD OF BUSINESS

Understanding the Mind Model allows complex personal or business dynamics to be observed without getting caught up in the dynamics. This is what allowed, for example, Ed Braithwaite to pull himself out of his job as a wall board finisher ("dry-waller") to own his company and then increase its income 10 times within three years. He never allowed himself to slip into someone else's definition of himself again. "The Mind Model," he said, "helped make everything *fit* into one, easy to manage, frame. It was my blueprint for looking at my life and keeping me on track."

Using the Mind Model allow updraft solutions to appear for every problem. It creates a menu of options at every turn. Downdraft thinking is easily identified and the entire team immediately understands that no solutions to anything occur in downdraft thinking. The focus shifts to becoming part of the solution rather than remaining part of the problem. The implicate order, family and cultural holodynes, comfort zone thinking and feelings, holodynes and our ability to change what we choose are all on the table when the mind model is used.

Assignment 63: Role-play a situation in which different departments in a company are negotiating for budget allotments. Who ends up with control of how much of the money and why?

Assignment 64: Replay the roles using the mind model. What difference did the use of the mind model make in the negotiation process? Was the final allotment changed? Discuss, make notes and share in your Holon.

Internal dialogues between managers, union representatives and others involved in any set of circumstances can be assessed from any position at the table of negotiations. In Manual IV, these processes are explored in more detail.

The Stages of Development Chart and the Bird's Eye View chart form valuable tools for team members in business. In the fifth manual, we will outline the six stages of natural development for each of the divisions of a normal business. Market driven, administrative, financial, personnel development and other aspects of business are considered as part of the whole dynamic. The entire potentialization process, as outlined in the first book Holodynamics (1990) and The Dance of Life (2005) make sense and help us produce extraordinary results.

D. TEAMING UP TO FOCUS ON POTENTIAL

The potentialization process applies the implicate order to the process of manifesting the potential in any given set of circumstances. It is so simple and so powerful that anyone can manifest whatever they want using the process. The best way to teach it is to use it in real-life situations. The experience of the process must precede teaching it. This is why those who want to be effective must first apply the processes before they seek to be consultants who guide others on the use of the processes.

Training allows a series of group experiences that deal with different dynamics with systems. In role-plays, holodynes can be triggered about business, money and making deals. These holodynes can then be processed and the participants are ready to do business on a more effective and mature basis. The roles can be played over and over by a single individual until s/he gets the solution or they can be played over and over by different individuals until everyone understands the dynamics.

Assignment 65: Role-play a business transaction where one person is negotiating to make above-fair-market profits.

E. THE BEING OF SYSTEM'S SYNERGY (BOSS)

We teach how to tap into the synergy inherent within the implicate order of systems. Holodynes emerge that control synergy. We call these the Beings of Systems Synergy (BOSS). Empowering the BOSS begins among the holodynes of the mind. We organize Round Tables so each person gains a new dimension of personal power and alignment with the FPS of the BOSS among the holodynes. Manual IV and V will give detailed training in these areas.

F. EMPOWERING THE BOSS AMONG HOLODYNES

Empowering the BOSS internally sets the stage for empowering the BOSS on the job. We teach how to empower the internal BOSS through tracking and other processes as outlined. We empower the BOSS on the JOB through skits, trust circles, potentializing and group projects. We use the empowered BOSS to potentialize groups, community systems, church groups, task teams, business divisions and any other system that is part of unfolding the potential of collective consciousness.

Empowering the BOSS can be accomplished by empowering the Team. Participants can learn to empower their BOSS when they team up to help empower a project. It can be any project, even empowering the seminars on unfolding potential. Successful action plans, deciding ways to team up, outreach to others, continued study and support groups are training on empowering the BOSS. Becoming an Advocate, a Consultant, Facilitator, Co-Presenter, Teacher or a Master Teacher, also empowers the BOSS.

Assignment 66: Discuss the processes necessary for potentializing seminars on Unfolding Potential. Use the potentializing process.

G. USING A PERSONAL PLANNER

In a very personal way, the Unfolding Potential Workbook, used as a complement in some Phase I Seminars is designed as extensions of the BOSS training. Also any workbooks (as, for example, Addiction Free Living, the Full Potential Self, Intimacy, etc.) are designed to lead up to empowering the BOSS. These lead to consultation services that show in detail how to implement principle driven business into daily management.

To this end, we encourage all participants, if they have not already done so, to begin to use a daily planner. In this way, the advice of their internal guides and of their Full Potential Self can be written down and put into their daily schedule.

Much like running a corporation, this internal corporation of the Round Table, made up of one's mature guides, meets on a regular daily basis and disseminates information, gives assignments and clarifies the dynamics of daily living. Much like taking notes in a corporate meeting, everyone has the opportunity to put into writing and into daily action, the information they have received from their guides. This can be accomplished very well through a daily time management process.

Assignment 67: Over the next year, keep a daily planner.

H. DYNAMIC MANAGEMENT: INTERNAL DIALOGUES AND STRATEGIC PLANNING.

When Holodynamics is applied to business dynamics, it is possible to recognize complex internal dialogues that are subconsciously controlling productivity, efficiency and the entire work process.

Using the potentializing process, it is possible to create a language and specific processes that make strategic planning both comprehensive and applicable. With these tools in hand, a new era of management emerges. A team-building, open, communicating corporate culture is cultivated where every individual is able to perform at his or her fullest potential possible. Corporate mentalities transform.

Jobs that are traditionally kept in-house, or within the company payrolls, are now contracted out to a population of workers who compete for the most effective, efficient way to accomplish the job required. New, better technology and more effective communication make possible a future in which every person become self-motivated and company conscious. Any company that remains insensitive to this coming Age of Information, cannot possibly compete in the future.

Assignment 68(optional): Plan a business that can be sold on the Web as part of the Web store. Use the Bird's-Eye View Chart and the Mind Model and other tools as presented in this training. Present the business preliminary plan to your team.

The name of the business is: _____

The product(s) are: _____

Details of the business are: _____

5. ALIGNING WITH PRINCIPLES

An empowered BOSS will reflect an internal integrity in any business. The Mind Model can be used to show how the six levels of development of consciousness, updraft and downdraft patterns, the critical choices and the ability to choose come together in principled living. It is that state of being in which a person aligns with the guiding principles of the implicate order and owns them as part of their personal nature.

This internal integrity spreads from among one's holodynes, into one's personality. Then it "catches on" in a synergistic way to produce the extra energy to get the job done in a coherent way. The team works together in a harmonic that can actually be felt by everyone. Enthusiasm increases; excitement pulses through the company; and people enjoy their work, care about each other, communicate honestly and deeply and become friends. Work is like family. People trust and create coherence together.

Integrity in business can only be achieved when the people are principle-driven. Management practices must be integritous. The courses on business dynamics are outlined in detail in the Academy.

Any project can be better understood and managed by taking it through the six levels. Marketing, sales, administration, finance, personnel development, accounting, and other aspects of company management can be integrated through the use of the potentialization and taken up through the six levels.

When people do this the results are an expanded, integrated, principle-driven leadership model which applies to any business. This approach provides everything necessary in the way of education, information, and training from micro to macro in business dynamics. It is a potentializing information store where the products and the BOSS are Holodynamic in nature and provide everything necessary to potentialize your life, your project and your company.

Doing business has changed dramatically in the last decade. Old polarizations that block success are now on the block themselves. The function of polarizations - how to resolve them, the thesis/antithesis/synthesis process, using the FPS, tracking and potentializing - create tools for transforming polarizations and harvesting the hidden power within every organization. These tools are now becoming available worldwide on the Web at the Holodynamic store.

Assignment 70: Create a shelf for your own project(s): Identify at least one service, technology, intellectual property or manufactured product that you envision could be on the shelf of a Web store. Outline how you envision it being of value and selling on the market.

Who would want to buy such a product? How would it be delivered? How would it be paid for? How much would it cost? How would you make money? What is your next step in making your Web shelf a reality?

A. POTENTIALIZING A PRINCIPLED-DRIVEN BUSINESS

Potentializing requires a certain harmonic, an inner integrity, within the business. This is the "I AM" quality of any business. Any business that is made up of people who have become the business is able to maintain principle-driven business processes and policies. Manual V outlines and demonstrates how the integrity of doing business and principled management are accomplished. These principles are taught in the Business Courses, introduced in Phase I and taught in detail in the BOSS courses.

Assignment 71: Identify three principles that drive a healthy business. Discuss.

B. ROLE-PLAYING RELATIONSHIP DYNAMICS

Role-playing is a process in which participants are instructed in taking a role and then playing that role as though it were real. The purpose of role-playing is to provide an exploring and learning environment that stimulates integration of thinking and feeling into a more effective state of being.

As participants we learn, through role-playing, to handle lifelike situations at every level of development and in a wide variety of situations. How to manage drug abuse, sex, disease and money are roles that integrate Level One. Role-plays on self-deception, lack of self-esteem and self-defeating behaviors are used to teach Level Two dynamics. Level Three, intimacy, triangle love affairs and communication roles are designed to increase the participant's ability to stay on course in relationships. At Level Four we use business roles and teaming up. Environmental issues, values and ethics are involved in Level Five roles and global issues are involved in Level Six.

Sometimes more than one level is involved in a single role-play. Usually we attempt to produce roles for which there is no solution unless one plays deep, honest and Holodynamically. Dozens of roles are outlined in this manual under the role-playing section.

Assignment 72: Create at least two role-play situations for EACH of the six levels. Write them out and include them in your journal.

C. USING INTUITIVE GUIDES IN BUSINESS

At each level of development, guides can be used to help create integration. The mature form of each holodyne can be invited to sit at the Round Table, within the Place of Peace and maintain an ongoing dialogue. This exchange of information can reflect the updraft of every level of the emerging consciousness. Guides can stimulate health and vitality, personal transformation and creativity, deep intimacy, team synergy, principle-driven integrity and expansion into universal oneness.

Setting up daily processes and tuning in at one's Round Table aligns particle and wave dynamics, accesses immature holodynes, puts everything together in a Place of Peace, allows the Full Potential Self to be involved in a conscious way and empowers integrity in all you do.

Discussing subjects at each of the six levels shows conceptually how a person becomes an extension of the living principles. This is usually accomplished in a business by having certain stories or metaphors that transmit the guiding principles of the company. In Manual IV, these metaphors and the principles they transmit will be explored in more detail. Those on the team who acknowledge "I am the business" are different than those that say "I need the business". Just as those who say "I AM LOVE" are in a different state of being than those who say "I NEED LOVE." Similarly, "I am abundance" is different that "I need more money."

Assignment 73: Discuss with your small group: What internal guides sit at your Round Table to help you with your business? Record your data in our journal.

6. UNIVERSALIZING

Potentializing begins within each individual. In order to potentialize anything it is necessary to recognize that everything is connected. One individual cannot be potentialized alone. We were not born alone and we cannot live alone or even die alone. We are part of one, whole, dynamic, living information system within a Holodynamic universe. The time comes in every conscious person's life when they realize that, to truly potentialize as a person, we must become involved the potentialization of each other, of our relationships, communities, countries and of the planet. That is to say we must become aligned with the quantum coherence of the greatest potential for life for this planet. Information is organized from micro (smallest) to macro (biggest). As we (a relatively micro part of the universe) *potentialize,* so goes the potentialization of the universe.

In order for the planet to reach its potential, it is necessary to first create the harmonic or the same potential within each of us. Our external world is created first within our own internal world. We have the power to organize internally. And we have the power to extend this internal integrity into our external world. Recognition of potential begins with the recognition of personal potential within and then the extension of this potential to others, systems, and into the world.

This micro-to-macro potentialization of the planet begins by creating a world of peace among the holodynes of own personal inner world of holodynes. There is a universal harmonic, a "sacred geometry" (see, for example, the work of Dan Winters) that resonates with such a clear field of information that people align with the information and immediately become beings of integrity and coherence. This is a state of being which reflects through the body personality (Full Potential Self) relationships (BOT) systems (BOSS) and through **the state of being** of everyone. It *resets the field* so the planet can come to coherence regarding its own potential.

In a state of coherence, the planet can potentialize. It is far more exciting to potentialize the planet and align with life's emergent possibilities than to create war. The Russian top military generals understood this in our first confrontation. "War is inevitable!" the general shouted. "War is not inevitable!" I shouted back. I went on to explain, "What is inevitable is that life will unfold its potential. Our moral and ethical responsibility is to help that potential unfold in our personal lives, our communities, our countries and in the world. That sir is inevitable!" He understood at once and, in that common harmonic of understanding, we became the best of friends.

War creates destruction of the networks that are necessary to potentialize the planet. Peace allows these networks to be intelligently designed and built. Communication systems, economic bonds, transportation and trade can be potentialized more fully when people are in quantum coherence with the deep implicate order of life at its fullest potential.

World potential is reflected through individual potential and individual potential is reflected through world potential.

Collective consciousness is made up of all its parts. It becomes "causal" because the holodynes that store the collective become self-preserving. They, like every living entity, want to survive. It becomes a force unto itself. People try to "manage" the collective by using mass media and various tactics for persuading people to believe in certain ways.

Assignment 74: List at least three ways the collective consciousness is managed in our society. Now list at least three ways the collective is managed in other cultures. Are there any differences? Discuss your findings.

Sometimes our government is managed by "crisis." Government programs often generate funding or movement of the public support by creating the impression of a crisis in oil, endangered species, stock market fluctuations, financial crisis, budget crisis, aids, cancer, heart disease, obesity (and a whole stream of other health concerns), housing, jobs, trade, and etc. Sometimes it appears as though there is a new crisis on the hour, every hour of every working day. The process itself generates personal crisis as citizens tend to revert to crisis-management processes used by the collective. This personal shift reverts back to the government and generates more collective management by crisis.

Assignment 75: Discuss: How many people does it take to shift the collective process of government? Outline how such a shift can be accomplished.

A. EVENT HORIZONS

Information organizes into stable systems called "event horizons" (Assim). All matter is able to hold itself in place because the information that makes up the matter is spinning in a harmonic that closes it off into a stable system. This "closing off" creates the boundaries between what is manifest and what does not become manifest. Atoms appear "separate" because the information has "collapsed" into a harmonic that cycles like a small hurricane and takes upon itself an identity. So every atom is a spinning set of information within an event horizon. Everything made of atoms in an event horizon.

Event horizons have an "updraft" and a "downdraft" spin. When the information updrafts ,the event horizon opens up and expands itself to include more information. It takes upon itself a positive valence that attracts other information systems. When the information downdrafts, the event horizon begins to collapse in upon itself. It begins to "die" in the sense that its manifest forms begins to dissolve back into the quantum potential field.

You and I are "event horizons" and, as such, we have a dark side (downdraft) that is continually collapsing and an expanding light side (updraft). This collapsing and expanding process functions universally. From the white and black holes within the microscopic quantum foam (Fred A. Wolfe), to the white and black holes of outer space, event horizons can be seen as the byproduct of warps or bends in light and the space time continuum that is related to gravitation fields. The balance of power between these two fields creates the stability of our atoms and structure, our personality and our consciousness. This extends into internal event horizons that determine our holodynes, how they relate and, in turn, control our own relationships.

Each event horizon, filled with the potential to expand or contract, extends into every aspect of our reality. By focusing upon this potential, we can align our lives so as to maximize our contribution to expand ourselves or constrict ourselves. Our focus determines our future, whether our physical reality expands or contracts. We can, for example, take the atomic weapons and the military might of the world - with all its poison gases, biological mutations, genetic manipulations, technological innovations, and use them to kill life on the planet. We certainly have the capacity to end all life on the planet right now, more than a thousand times, if we so choose. On the other hand, we also hold within our hands the capability of the potentialization of the planet into a new era of enlightenment.

The interesting aspect of reality is that each of us, every single person, holds the key to which way the future will be shaped. One person can reset the entire field. In fact, personal potentialization is a prerequisite to world potentialization. The Place of Peace, Round Table, intuitive guides from every dimension of life and regular guidance sessions that are based upon mature principles, processes and organizational structure *empower* each individual to become part of the new resonating field for world peace and potentialization of the planet.

The inner world of the mind reflects into the outer world. We resonate with certain frequencies that are controlled by our holodynes and designed to create updraft or downdraft dynamics. There are certain skills - real skills - we can learn by which this transformation takes place from micro to macro, from within the mind among the holodynes, through the personality, into relationships, systems, principled living and into life as a whole.

Thousands and thousands of people have made the choice. What choice? The choice to align with their Full Potential Self and "take the course" that leads to expansion of awareness, love, peace and prosperity. The choice that leads to harmonic coherence with life potential. It is the most important, deepest, most meaningful and powerful choice a person can make. It is a choice for life. It is the choice to potentialize.

Potentialization begins with the personal choice to choose life. The choice becomes clear. We each get to choose rational/intuitive perception, updraft/downdraft processes, any stage of development for our living, and how to use the life force. Choice affects personal power. We can use our ISP, learn to focus clearly, use our personal influence to collapse the wave and create the kind of world we want. Our event horizon can expands. We can all "pop" through into a new dimension of consciousness.

When we choose, even in subtle ways, to downdraft the dynamics, we sink back into the collapse of our personal event horizon. Our consciousness becomes trapped within old patterns and old holodynes. We begin to die. When one person collapses their event horizon, the collective event horizon also begins to collapse.

Assignment 76: What triggers downdraft dynamics in your life? Create a "map" or a "cluster" of what happens when the trigger is pulled? Discuss.

In physics, event horizons describe reality. That is -

1. Everything is made of information in motion;
2. There are three forms of matter: *waves, standing waves (particles)* and *presence;*
3. These three types of forms give rise to every set of circumstances of life;
4. Every set of circumstances is driven by potential;
5. All information is connected even though we may not be able to measure the connections from within our particular set of circumstances or event horizons;
6. There is an implicate order to all information systems; and
7. Information systems emerge as unique within a unified field.

The unique information system with a field is contained within an event horizon.

In biological systems, all life forms are also made of information in motion:

1. Consciousness emerges as information enters the microtubules.
2. There it is spun into holodynes as self-organizing and self-sustaining information systems.
3. Holodynes control every body function, its coherence and every aspect of consciousness.
4. Mechanisms of biological function have aspects of wave, particle and presence.
5. Coherence in biological systems is Holodynamic.

At each level of organization, each biological system and each subsystem is considered to exist within an event horizon. That is, for example, each cell has its own event horizon. Each bacteria, virus, and molecule has its own event horizon, even thought it may be contained within a larger event horizon. These subsystems are referred to as *holon* nested within a larger system. Humans have millions of such holons within their bodies and even more within their holodynes.

In psychology, information *polarizes*:

1. Information systems spin with "upward" direction or "downward" direction. Information systems have implosive and explosive dynamics.
2. Games of life are the result of polarizations. Male/female, good/bad, dominant/submission, close/distant, rich/poor, have/have-not, knowledge/ignorance, victim/perpetuator/rescuer, employer/employee/consultant/ etc. are the result of *particle* and *wave* dynamics. Problems result because polarization games are driven by potential solutions.
3. Solutions are found in presence.

Presence permits you to consciously remove yourself from the event horizon of the game being played. If you do not remove yourself from the event horizon, you cannot comprehend the dimension from which solutions are manifest so you cannot solve the problem. This is why people continue, generation after generation, to have the same problems.

Spirituality alludes to *Presence* wherein a person *integrates* information allowing for the emergence of a *new* event horizon:

1. Presence is to gain access to the *source* of information.
2. The source of information is inclusive, beyond the confines of polarization games.
3. *Alignment* with presence creates new information fields.
4. Blocks to presence can be *potentialized* by accessing the holodynes that are holding the event horizon in place. The processes of Holodynamics, such as *tracking, reliving* and *preliving,* create new event horizons.
5. Those who practice religion may be locked into event horizons that do not permit them to solve problems faced by their community even though they may believe in solving problems. Beliefs about spirituality can be divinized and thus rendered powerless.

Every problem facing the planet is *caused by the solutions* embedded within the implicate order and available to those who access *presence*. Problems can be potentialized. It is a matter of bringing the situation to its fullest potential.

In the practical world of reality, people seek to solve their problems. For this reason, the International Academy of Holodynamics sponsors courses that teach what is known from a context of using this information to solve the problems we face and unfold our future potential together. These courses are based upon the best of the current sciences integrated into a practical, what-works approach that has been tested and proven effective in solving even the most complex problems on the planet.

Everyone has their own unique event horizons. We invite you to learn both the academic information and develop the skills necessary so that you can become part of creating a more sustainable future for yourself and for the planet. This means becoming an Advocate. As an Advocate, you begin the process and, as you pass through the Circles of Success, not only will you learn to unfold your own potential but you will also learn to teach others to do the same. We encourage you to organize a Holon or study group and *take the course.*

B. THE POWER OF CHOICE

When Francis refused to join in the family fun at Lake Powell, in southern Utah, she felt isolated and inadequate. She wanted to join in but she had a life-long phobia that would not allow her to enter the water. When we tracked her phobia, she recalled an incident when she was 3 years old and had almost drowned in a neighbor's swimming pool. She did not want to drown. She wanted to live a full and productive life. Once she accessed the fears of her 3 year-old child (still active holodynes in her memory banks), she was able to relive the process through the eyes of her Full Potential Self, understand what her fears wanted, and transform them. Not only did her fear of water disappear completely, but her fears of sex and intimacy, taking charge of situations, as well as a long line of inhibitions, soon joined the transformation train. It was her choice.

Choice actively impacts the quantum wave. In doing so, it impacts the past, present and future. It impacts parallel worlds. These parallel worlds create many of the dynamics that most cloud our conscious awareness. When you choose to access your holodynes, you enter into the deeper arenas of information and it is within these depths where information fields exist that control how energy is organized. It is not just a matter of the human mind. It is a matter of how reality is organized in a conscious universe.

This does not mean one person can rush out and change the color of the sky to green. The implicate order is complex, and matter appears as it does because we are all in *coalition* with one another. It is a covenant we all made. All consciousness agreed. A brick looks like a brick, feels like a brick and weighs what a brick weighs. In reality, that brick is a holographic projection made of endless bubbles (event horizons). Each is in quantum coherence with the others. This means that each is in correlation with us as well. So when we look at the brick, pick it up and cement it into the wall, it stays there, acting like a brick. A brick keeps its agreement to remain a brick until some new information interjects and shifts its field dynamics.

Assignment 77: Discuss: What is "the covenant"? How does the covenant affect reality? How can we affect the covenant?

C. THE FUTURE NOW

We can create the future now. We can visit the future, experience it in great detail and bring that information back into the present. We can heal all dimensions that which are blocking the unfolding of potential. We can actually create the future now. Many scientific discoveries, breakthrough technologies and quantum leaps in consciousness have occurred when dedicated men and women have focused on the future, gone there in their imaginations and found the answers to their questions.

Read the story of Einstein's discovery of the relationship between mass and momentum, his famous e=mc2. Study Jonas Salk's explanation of how he found the Salk vaccine that cured polio. The Benzene ring, the Bessemer converter (the basis of mass produced steel) and many other inventions, including Tesla's work in electronics (that produced most of our electrical world), are all examples of great people who dared to enter hyperspace, access the future and bring back information. Every citizen of the planet Earth can do the same. There are no "off-limits" signs keeping anyone from qualifying for being a genius. The future can be now for any person who chooses, goes to his Place of Peace, calls upon his Full Potential Self and asks what is going to occur that has meaning for himself.

Exercise 78: What sense of the future do you have? Can you recall a specific event in which you knew something was going to happen before it actually occurred? How did you get it? How did it help you in the present? How can you enhance this skill? Write it down in your journal and discuss it with your Holon.

D. CRITICAL MASS

It is said that it takes *critical mass* to potentialize some things. Critical mass refers to the necessary harmonic energy to shift a field. The field is conditioned within certain event horizon boundaries. To impact these boundaries requires input of potential energy sufficient to move from one state to another. In one sense, motors provide the critical mass of energy to create motion. This is what moves cars, trains and planes. It built the Industrial Age. But what kind of critical mass must be present to move people?

There are different kinds of critical mass but the principle remains the same. Peace, for example, must have a critical mass that allows new dynamics that are more powerful than war dynamics. Choice creates the energy to establish peace processes when conflict arises. Those who choose peace processes in the face of conflict, become part of the solution only when they transform the war field. They are, in reality, building a new field. It is the potential field that people were seeking when they went to war. With the right focus, one person has the critical mass to shift an entire field.

Assignment 79: Discuss: Why do people go to war? Write your perception and discuss it with your Holon.

E. THE ROUND TABLE PROCESS

In order to create an event horizon that resonates with the harmonics of peace, it is necessary to create peace among your internal world. This means peace among your holodynes. Those who establish a Place of Peace and stay aligned with that state of being are soon confronted with holodynes that are at war with each other and cause warring behavior in the lives of all those who host them. One very successful way to participate in the ongoing process of peace is to establish a Round Table in your Place of Peace. This can symbolize a meeting place for all holodynes, whether at war or at peace, whether mature or immature. All can meet, negotiate, communicate, share their intentions and allow for mutual growth.

The processes for creating a Round Table are taught in the Unfolding Potential Seminars. Basically, it is just a matter of using your imagination to visualize such a table. This is an instant recall image at which sits your Full Potential Self and any other inner guides.

Assignment 80: Create a Round Table in your Place of Peace. Draw out the members you have chosen to sit with you at your Round Table. Is your Full Potential Self among them? Share with your Holon.

F. BUILDING THE FIELD

It requires skill to build a field. We teach the essential skills required for shifting the field because the skills must be taught. That's why Marty Sullivan, in the San Francisco Bay area, contends he never would have become a minister without having the skills taught in Holodynamics. That's why Jeannie Low never would have known how to approach gang members on the streets of Los Angeles and how so many people have learned to relate more effectively in their deepest and most intimate relationships.

You can extend your influence and your own personal potential by helping others gain these same skills. This manual is written to help you learn to hone and teach these skills. Prepare yourself to teach by first learning the skills and practicing them in your own personal life. Then become certified to teach. By becoming certified, you give yourself permission to test your own skill development.

Certification insures quality and depth of skill development. Certification shows you have demonstrated your commitment to make a difference, to prepare yourself professionally to extend this knowledge and this technology into the world. Starting with micro fields, or those dealing with personal holodynes, we extend out into more and more macro fields.

With practice, you become an Advocate, Consultant, Facilitator, Presenter, Teacher and then a Master Teacher. You become a front liner, a citizen ambassador for shifting the field for potentialization of the planet.

Assignment 81: Discuss what field you would like to see transformed. Outline a plan that can accomplish this transformation. What part will you play in the transformation? How will you proceed? What will be the results? Share with your Holon.

The objective of these exercises is to explore the state of being present within a specific situation. These exercises are exploratory, not judgmental. They are designed to invite participants into a greater awareness of when they are present and when they are not present. The questions and processes will amplify sensitivity to how little they have been present, the ways they have been absent, the causes behind these absences (holodynes) and how to take control of their lives. With participant aware of these causes, they will be able to better access, track, and transform the holodynes that are distracting and controlling them.

In order to participate in these exercises, participants must be familiar with stepping beyond the situation and into a self-observation position. This includes having a Place of Peace, a Round Table, and a relationship with one's Full Potential Self as taught in the Holodynamic courses. At any given moment, the participant can choose to shift one's focus, go into a state of being at peace, sit at the Round Table and consult with one's Full Potential Self. It is stepping beyond being controlled by the situation (or its holodynes) and observing with the help of one's Full Potential Self.

The Participant should be familiar with the process of accessing one's holodynes, communicating, finding the holodyne's potential and setting a field so the holodyne will transform itself into its fullest potential.

Usually such a transformation aligns the energy and power of the holodyne with one's Full Potential Self. This alignment releases the resistance and frees the person to focus fully on what is wanted. Sometimes, however, the holodyne is part of a larger event horizon. Thus the Participant may be required to identify the entire event horizon and transform it using a similar process or, if it is a wider, more ancient information system, it may require a relive/prelive process. These processes are taught in Holodynamic introductory courses and participants should be familiar with them before doing this exercise.

Controlling holodynes comes from an event horizon within which holodynes "live" and control the participant's behavior. Identifying the holodynes and their event horizons increases the participants' field of information so they can distinguish between their focus and their interference from holodynes. They can then choose to transform the interference that distract them from their chosen behavior. This increases their ability to be present and expand awareness of self as they experience each exercise.

CHAPTER SEVEN

HOW TO POTENTIALIZE A SEMINAR

W HY WOULD AN ENTIRE CHAPTER BE DEVOTED TO POTENTIALIZING A SEMI-
NAR? Because teaching unfolding potential can be part of the celebration of life
for an Advocate. The key to understanding life and manifesting what you want is
potentializing. Manifesting potential is the essence of life itself. Your life is about
unfolding your potential. The transfer of potential energy to kinetic energy and the transfer of
the quantum field into conscious reality are all part of the field dynamics by which life and *we* as
humans have our being. Life is the most powerful force on earth and, in its emergence, we unfold. Within this matrix we are faced with a series of challenges that we must face and these
challenges can only be solved by teaching potentializing.

The implicate order by which life unfolds indicates there are certain steps to potentializing. These steps follow the six stages of growth of the implicate order. These are outlined in the
Circles of Success and they have been tested over and over in the course of our exploration, which
led to the potentializing program. The six steps will be outlined below but only the first step is
considered in detail in this, the first manual on the Holodynamic State of Being. This information is what you need to know in order to become an Advocate/Teacher. Each step is covered
in detail in each of the certification manuals. Each level of certification reflects an emerging order of your own potentialization as a Holodynamist.

FOCUS ON THE POTENTIAL OF THE SEMINAR

Focus begins the process of potentializing. In a sense, everything we do in the Unfolding Potential course is geared to identifying what potential we want to unfold. Working within
the boundary conditions of reality, we potentialize what we want. We begin with focus and we
actually facilitate the unfolding of that potential we want. We can practice here, in this text, by
unfolding the teaching of potentializing. We advocate potentializing. In the seminars on potentializing, the Presenter, by thought and action, models such potentializing. We begin by advocating the potentializing the seminar itself.

The presenter is the master Potentializer of the seminar. You can use the potentializing
process to potentialize each seminar as a project. Long before you step onto the Presenter's role
you must team up to put the seminar through the potentializing process. The general potentialization process follows the six steps, as outlined in Addendum E.

You will note that the potentializing process uses the Mind Model. The introductory
course, Phase I, follows the six steps of potentializing and it uses the Mind Model. The Potentializing chart gives us an icon to remind us of the processes inherent within each step. First we

focus on potential. Then, once we identify what we choose, we check out that choice within the context of the Mind Model.

Check List One:

- Is the potential of choice a rational, particle or Holodynamic choice? Is it an emotional, wave dynamic? Is it Holodynamic?

- What holodynes are governing the choice?

- Are the holodynes mature or immature, updraft or downdraft?

- At what level of the implicate order are these holodynes manifesting? Are they focused on physical reality or personal development? Are they relationship-oriented or systems-attached? Are they principle driven or universal?

- What energy level is involved in each holodyne? What potential lies inherent within it?

- These are typical exploration questions regarding your focus on what is wanted.

Check List Two: Call upon your Full Potential Self.

- Ask for guidance so that your choice can be integrated into all dimensions of your own potential.

- Repeat Step One. Only this time, ask the questions of your Full Potential Self and explore the answers deeply. Does your Full Potential Self agree with your own conclusions reached in Step One?

- What adjustments are necessary in order to be in coherence?

Check List Three: Call upon the Full Potential Self of your most intimate team members who will be helping unfold the potential of choice.

- Take the discussion through Step One again.

- Do their Full Potential Selves all agree?

- Is there any more alignment necessary in order to have coherence?

Check List Four: Call upon or create the Fullest Potential for the team as a body. Allow the entity of the project to emerge and have the entity sit at your Round Table and go through Step one.

- Does the information remain coherent?

- Are any more adjustments necessary in the process of unfolding the potential of the project?

Check List Five: Identify the guiding principles for the project which is being potentialized. Take these principles through Step one again using the Mind Model.

- What guiding principles will the team adopt as their own?

- Do all of the FPSs at the Round Table agree?

- Are any adjustments necessary?

Check List Six: Ask the universe to send a representative to your Round Table who can guide your team and the project so that it aligns with the greatest potential for everything involved.

- What represents the highest potential of the project?

- Will a representative (holodyne) sit at your Round Table to give the highest potential of the project a voice?

- Does the new entity align with all other FPSs at the table?

- Are any adjustments necessary?

The processes and principles taught in this course are enfolded within these six steps and are necessary in order to create your own reality and get what you want in a project you want to potentialize. In the case of the seminar or in such a process of potentializing your own certification, take the steps. Potentialize your seminar!

Here are some guidelines for the team to use as a guide in potentializing a seminar:

BEFORE THE SEMINAR BEGINS

Before the seminar begins, an effective Presenter will focus on the details of what is wanted in the seminar. Consider some of the following details:

1. Creating the maximum physical arena for learning
2. Aligning personal integrity and conceptual clarity with course content
3. Aligning team members, coordinators, networkers, facilitators and participants
4. Orchestrating the whole event from start to finish
5. The principles, processes and events as an integrated whole dynamic
6. Extension into areas of potential growth

Consider this process of potentializing the course, in conjunction with others. Team up with the Coordinators, Facilitator, Networkers and Marketing teams. Constantly seek feedback from participants. Be in harmony with what this seminar is supposed to do. Make sure the seminar itself "walks its talk."

Every experience must be integrated into this process. A Master Presenter will not only rationally understand how this is done, but will be *continually, intuitively* doing this no matter what level of patterning is brought before the group.

CREATING A MAXIMUM LEARNING ENVIRONMENT

Any seminar should create a maximum learning environment for its participants. Using the Mind Model, we begin at level one, physical setting.

A. PHYSICAL SETTING

In order to create a clear focus and an environment for maximal learning, you must have as few distractions as possible and as many of the necessary tools for *learning as* are available. For example:

a. **CHAIRS**: Chairs are in a semicircle or in classroom style to begin with. The objective here is to have each person so that they can feel comfortable but begin to experience the others in the class.

b. **SOUND**: It is essential that everyone hear. For groups of more than 50, have at least three microphones - one for the Presenter and two hand mikes for traveling. It is best to have cordless mikes because the cords can become a major distraction to the learning process. Set up a good speaker system and make sure it works before the meeting begins. Have both a tape player and a tape recorder. If you are going to tape each session, be sure you have enough tapes for the hours involved and someone to handle the sound system. Any course requires the ability to play tape-recorded music for mind journeys. Be sure that an adequate sound system is in place well before the meeting begins.

c. **REGISTRATION**: All registration forms and money-intake management systems must be in place well before the seminar begins. Proper staffing, control and information exchange is necessary. This material is available in the Coordinator's Handbook.

d. **REMOVE DISTRACTIONS**: The complete environment must be conducive to teaching. Distractions must be kept to a minimum, and everything must demonstrate potentialization.

PERSONAL INTEGRITY AND MASTERY OF TEACHING

Before you can teach something, you must be practicing it yourself. Here are some examples:

A. **HAVE A WORKING KNOWLEDGE OF WHAT TO TEACH:** The ability to access and implement information from the intuitive mind and then interpret that information accurately and transform what needs to be transformed allows you to become empowered as a teacher using your full intuitive powers.

B. **MAINTAIN INDIVIDUALITY:** The ability to maintain your own uniqueness in the garden of different situations or in different roles (as in the Holodynamic program as an Advocate, Consultant, Facilitator, Team Teacher, Presenter or a Master Teacher). Your own personal special gifts allow you to generate results as a each person to be a generative, pro-active agent for any group or individual with whom one is in contact.

C. **DISCRETE DISCLOSURE:** The ability to set personal issues aside, to shift into a mature presenting mode and allow the enlightened intuitive shaking of personal dynamics which enhance the education process.

D. **APPLICATION OF THE PROCESSES:** The application of the processes refers to potentializing the potential. It shows up as your ability to apply the processes in the educational arena; to acknowledge the downdraft holodynes in all of us and specifically within one's self; to identify the consequences for maintaining such a state of being; and then transform the holodynes and shift the fields involved. The results of potentializing show up as unfolding the potential of such states.

E. **CENTERING:** The ability to be centered on one's Full Potential Self. A state of being in coherence, integrity and harmony. Also, to go where the people are, to enter into the flow of their own life energy, access their Full Potential Self and center in on those issues which will aid their progression the most.

F. **PHASE SPACING:** In electronics, when one wave is resonating out of phase with another, the process of moving the wave into harmony by changing the phase is called *phase spacing*. In life, the act of removing a set of circumstances into another quantum state or *phase* is also called *phase spacing*. It is like taking an instrument and tuning it so it plays in harmony with the orchestra. When you use the Mind Model as a reference, you can align any situation with your Full Potential Self and focus on the harmonic of the fullest possible potential for that situation. This is called *phase spacing*. In other words, you can tune in to any situation by moving your consciousness into a superposition - being both *in* and *out* of the situation at the same time - and this position allows you to unfold the potential more effectively.

G. **COMMITMENT:** The ability to *stay with* a person, a group or an issue until resolution is achieved or potential is unfolded. This also includes the ability to commit to be there for one's self, for the processes and principles of Unfolding Potential, for a group, for a program and for the mission purpose, which brings people into community.

H. **GLOBAL HARMONY**: The ability to be flexible, a part of the larger whole as a unit thereof. This includes being able to teach in any location, with any other presenter, to add one's strengths and gifts to those of any other(s), and to give up ownership of any special location or people. As a planetary citizen, one becomes a living part of the universe to help potentialize the planet.

THE POWER TO FOCUS

There are special aspects to focusing which are essential to effectiveness. These include -

A. **BE PRESENT.** This is a course on being present so you, the teacher, must begin with *presence*;

B. **FOCUS ON POTENTIAL.** Your focus is determined by the field of information that controls your holographic screens. Being aligned with your Full Potential Self assures your focus will be open, able to sense the whole dynamic and thus able to respond with the greatest amount of effectiveness;

C. **USE YOUR INTUITION.** You will be able to access both your intuitive experiences and following through with your rational explanations. You are what you advocate;

D. **INTEGRATE.** By integrating what your are facing in the class, you gain access to the dimensions that are hidden beneath the conscious awareness of the participants;

E. **BOND WITH THOSE IN THE CLASS.** When teaching a seminar, focus on the dimensions that produce the best results. Bonding is one of these dimensions. Teach the bonding processes and set the example for others to follow. This is real teaching; and

F. **FOLLOW-UP.** The class is not just an event; it is part of an ongoing process of potentializing. Once you have accepted the role of teacher, you are now responsible to set the example and follow through on potentializing each person who entered you class. You must teach the sequences of following through. This is a fail-free experience. Become the potentializer.

THE POWER OF INTUITION

In boxing you are taught to lead with your left and follow through with your right. In teaching you lead with your right and follow through with your left. That is, you start with an intuitive experience and then follow through with an **explanation.** To begin the seminars, an intuitive experience on focusing usually begins the whole process.

A. STARTING THE SEMINAR

Begin on time. Make sure your meetings begin on time. One way to begin is to have *sit-down music* and explain to the group that each meeting will begin with something which sets the style and mood you want for the course. Generally "upbeat" music gets a group moving and, in principle, music can be used to get the whole group emotionally involved from the start. The idea is that *when* the music ends everyone can be in their seats, in a participating mood, and ready to go. In this way you can save much time, which otherwise might be spent in random discussion rather than in planned group experiences.

B. PRIOR NOTICE:

Have door attendants. Have the small group leaders act as door attendants and inform each participant as they enter that they must be in their seats by the time the music stops. There are other options at this point. You may want to make it interesting for participants right away by suggesting to them, as they enter the room, that they not sit next to anyone they know. Usually the area coordinator will begin by giving the whole group a welcome to the unfolding potential seminars.

C. INTRODUCING THE PRESENTER:

Usually the area coordinator will introduce the Presenter. This can be done in many ways and sets the tone for the whole course. Personal histories, personal stories, resumes and such are usually kept to a minimum because the course does not center on the Presenter. It is usually enough for them to know "Your presenter(s) for the course will be … and give the name of the Presenter(s).

D. TELL A STORY:

One interesting way to begin is to tell a story. Presenters must realize that telling a story is an art and has many dimensions to it. It is an excellent way to get the course started on time and keep people's interest.

E. GET TO KNOW THE PARTICIPANTS:

Introducing people to each other can be a crucial turning point for the course. How you present the initial group interaction has a lot to do with what happens from then on, because it *imprints* how the game is to be played in many people's minds.

"WHAT DO YOU WANT?" You might start right out with: "What is it you want?" This can be from the course, in life, or in anything else. This begins the focus for the class in which participants learn to focus clearly on what they want. This also can be integrated into the quantum wave and how to potentialize.

Write each response on a large white easel paper and, when the paper is full, tape it on the wall. Fill as many sheets as it takes. Do not allow this to drag on too long but get the main wishes of the group up on the wall. This becomes the focus of the seminar. An example of "focusing" on what you want.

Explain to the class that **this is at least a 30-day course.** Over the next 30 days, at least, you will be working together to help each other hold the field and get what you want.

THE QUANTUM WAVE

Draw a wave upon the board. Explain that locked within the quantum wave is a certain *probability*. We call this the potential of the wave. We are at point "a" and we want to get to point "be" (draw point *a* and point *be* on the wave). In order to get there, we must **focus.**

Focus is a two-way street. Our senses send information *out* as well as take it *in*. Mechanists believe it's only input. Those who understand wave dynamics and quantum mechanics know that when you observe something, you affect it.

It's like each of us hold within our hand a cup. We focus upon the ocean of potential and we take our cup and dip it in and cause the thing we want to materialize.

OPTION: Have an aquarium present and a cup. Show how, when you dip the cup in, it causes the wave to collapse into the hole made by the cup. This is what scientists call "the collapse of the wave function."

OPTION: Have someone hold a rope. Take one end and cause a pulse to run down the rope by whipping it. This pulse is like a potential in the wave. It is a *probability*. When you focus upon the pulse and make it go in a circle, it causes it to become a standing wave or a separate physical reality.

Some of the reasons focusing is important include the following:

1. The quantum potential field is dynamic and interlaced with intelligent responsiveness. All reality, as we experience it with our senses, emerges from this field.
2. Focusing on a specific potential creates an *echo* effect upon the wave. Holding a clear focus *pops* the wave, or *collapses it*, so you manifest what you want.
3. Holodynes are the *carriers* or *transmitters* of information from your consciousness to the wave. Focusing on your holodynes is vital because they *hold* the field.
4. Intuitive Sensory Perception is necessary to access holodynes and influence their growth. When you use your ISP and focus, you can access your holodynes.
5. The *master* of all your holodynes is your Full Potential Self.
6. By controlling holodynes you can control potentialization. Sometimes this takes collective group action. The more complex the field, the more holodynes are involved and the more focus it takes to transform the field.
7. The Mind Model and the processes taught in this course will teach you to focus, master your holodynes, own your personal power, shift the field and potentialize what you want out of life.
8. Bonding between holodynes within the mind, as in the Round Table processes, between partners in the course, among small group members and in the larger group,

and then extending the bonding into the community, provides the necessary field dynamics to shift and hold the field for any endeavor.

9. The more complex the field, the more focus the people must have to hold it.

This is where the seminar gets really interesting because the main focus of the seminar is on the *people* who attend. It's *their* seminar. You will focus on what they want and what blocks them from getting what they want. You will be focusing on their holodynes and teaching them to transform their blocks into new sources of energy and information.

You will be focusing on how they can potentialize their lives and, ultimately, you will be focusing on solving the complex problems and meeting the great challenges of our day. The Seminar creates a learning environment so that each person can learn to be successful in each Circle of Success.

The next chapter outlines in brief the focus of the Unfolding Potential Seminar. The Presenters will teach you the specifics of each section of the course. What seminars do, in a practical way, is create a learning environment so that you and your friends can learn to unfold the magnificent potential that rests within.

CHAPTER EIGHT

AN OVERVIEW OF THE COURSE ON UNFOLDING POTENTIAL

T HE FOLLOWING IS A BRIEF OVERVIEW OF A TYPICAL INTRODUCTORY COURSE ON the Holodynamics of unfolding potential. It is meant for reference use only so you can keep track of where the course in going. Each of the manuals that make up this series of manuals, will add to the understanding and give specific experiences that show examples of how these subjects are usually taught and how they apply to solving complex problems. This class lays the foundation for what is to come.

SECTION ONE: THE FULL POTENTIAL SELF

Introduction

> Welcome.
> Who are you?
> What do you want?

Potential

> Everything is driven by potential.
>> The first premise of quantum physics
>>> Electron formation according to potential
>>> Experiments with photon guns and particle/wave dynamics
>>> Geometric harmonics
> Unfolding potential in people
> Each person is empowered by a Full Potential Self
> Every problem is caused by its solution.

The Full Potential Self

> Perception: how our senses input information
>> The human senses
>> Fine grained and gross grained screens of the senses
>> The holographic dimension
>> EPR experiment, quantum coherence and control of the screens
> Accessing information using Intuitive Sensory Perception
> Accessing the Full Potential Self
> Accessing the FPS of others
> Making the commitment to "take the course" of the FPS

Bonding

Relating FPS to FPS.

SECTION TWO: THE POTENTIALIZATION PROCESS

The Covenant

Holodynamic reality: a covenant among FPSs
> The conscious universe
>> The holographic paradigm about physical matter
>> Holographic memory
> The Mind Model
>> The Holodynamic model of the universe

Bonding

Bonding as an Alignment with the Full Potential Self
> Bonding Conscious Self to FPS
> Rational and intuitive aspects of bonding
> Levels of maturity in bonding
> Empowering bonding experientially
>> Experiencing the room
>> Choosing a partner
>> Intuitive bonding
>> Organizing small groups

Blocks to Unfolding Potential

Getting from A to B.
> Sculpturing dynamics

Holodynes

Self Organizing Information Systems within the Microtubules
> Everything is made of information.
> Information organizes in three patterns.
>> Particle leads to rational thinking.
>> Wave leads to emotional dynamics.
>> Holodynamics leads to conscious choice.
> The six stages of the implicate order

Tracking as potentialization of holodynes

The six steps of tracking
> Tracking experiences with partners

Role-playing holodynes
Tracking and re-role playing

Clustering as potentialization of groups of holodynes

How to cluster complex situation dynamics
Accessing Positive Intent
Your Place of Peace
Full Potential Self exercises
Group Full Potential Self exercises
The Six Levels of Bonding

SECTION THREE: APPLICATIONS OF POTENTIALIZATION

Six Levels of Potentializing

Physical
Dealing with disease, energy and prosperity
Personal
Unfolding personal potential
Overcoming family and cultural blocks
Unfolding creative potential
Interpersonal
Intimacy and the Being of Togetherness
Intimacy Courses
Family dynamics
Social, cultural, and religious dynamics
Comfort Zone holodynes
Developing a support team
Overcoming collective pathology
Principles, morals, ethics and spirituality
Principle-driven living
Owning and becoming
Universal consciousness
Attuned knowing, loving oneness

Living a dynamic life through potentializing

Role-playing in daily dynamics
Potentializing external systems

Field Dynamics

Time-lines
Quantum Potential Fields

Mastering Vertical Dynamics

Genetic coding
Stages of the Life Cycle
Family Fields

Exploring Genograms

Transgenerational Patterns
Creating a Genogram
Using a Genogram

Creating Collages

Pictorial Patterning
Geometric Harmonics

The Principles and Processes of Relives

Accessing the Past
Using Guides
Restructuring the Information Fields

The Principles and Processes of Prelives

Accessing the Future
Integration with the Present
Unfolding Potential.

The Ethics of a Participant

SECTION SIX: GLOBAL DYNAMICS

The International Academy of Holodynamics

Accreditation of Courses in Holodynamic
Recognition of Certification
International Networking

Other Countries:

How to organize a branch of the Academy in your Country

Other Courses

How to create new materials
The process of accrediting new materials
Translation, marketing and management

Professional Centers

Teaching Teachers to Teach in a Modern World
Families and Communities
Business and Industry Courses
Programs for expansion

Identification of Potential Projects

Types of Projects
Roster of Masters
Teaming up

The Master's Council

The duties of the Council
Your responsibility to serve
The Association of Professionals
The International Conference
The Internet, WWW, e-mail and video conferencing
The Future

Sponsoring Others

The professional responsibility
The implications of the Code of Ethics
Following through
Criteria for success
Maintaining an ongoing relationship

Materials for the Presenter

Professional Code of Ethics
Personal log of certification requirements
Sponsor sheet

Holon Organization

Creating a local support group
Registration with the Central Office
Obtaining Materials for study

Activities and Projects
Global Networking

THE LEARNING ENVIRONMENT

My life was blessed with a learning environment within my own home. It never occurred to me until much later in life how much freedom I had and how much encouragement I got to explore and learn everything I could.

I was born in Canada and I remember a great snowfall when I was 5 years old. I got bundled up in my warmest outfit and went out into the snow. It was almost over my head and made of light powder.

I decided to roll down the hill behind our house. So I rolled and rolled in the snow. It was lots of fun. When I got to the bottom of the hill, I discovered the stream had frozen solid and the wind had blown the powdered snow clear from the ice. I walked along on the ice looking down through it into the almost clear, frozen water.

Suddenly I came upon a fish frozen in the ice! I was so excited. I climbed all the way back up the hill. I found my father's hatchet and a pail and went all the way down the hill again. Then, very carefully, I chipped the ice containing the fish out of its stream bed. I put the chunk of ice with the fish frozen in it into the bucket and then carried everything all the way back up the hill.

My mother watched all this with an attitude of wonder and amazement that matched my own excitement. I think she was actually glad to see me so involved in the learning process. We put the pail with the fish in the kitchen and soon the ice melted. To my surprise the fish was alive in the water! It began swimming around inside the bucket!

Much later in my life, when people seemed so immobile in their positions, I never forgot that just because something is frozen doesn't mean it has to be dead.

At a very young age, I became aware that a learning environment is a field of love in which life and all its possibilities are there to be explored.

Those who serve as *Advocates* make a commitment to create an environment where the potential of every situation can be explored so as to *unfold its potential*, encourage it to *take form* and to *hold a field* in which each person can reach their fullest possible potential. Sometimes it means just creating a warm enough environment so they can "thaw out" to new possibilities. All it takes is someone who can advocate enough faith to walk with them as they unfold.

When you sense you have mastered this skill, complete the necessary academic and field experience requirements and have a Sponsor present you as a candidate for Consultant. I congratulate you on taking this life-generating step.

Appendix A

Steps To Certification

The International Academy of Holodynamics offers courses and, upon successful completion, a graduate receives a Certificate of Graduation from that course. There are six natural steps to certification. There are referred to as the Circles of Success in the Academy. Each circle has its own training program, manual and requirements. All seven circles are sequential. The first circle is for **Advocates.** Advocates are those people who are committed to *taking the course of their Full Potential Self.* Advocates pledge to manifest their fullest potential in their personal lives and in the program. They *advocate* the Holodynamic view of reality and support the Academy and its program. Advocates learn its basic concepts and processes and support introducing people into the program.

The second Circle of Success is taken by **Consultants.** In order to certify as a Consultant, you must learn the first five processes of Holodynamics: Place of Peace, Full Potential Self, Round Table, Tracking and Potentializing. One you have mastered these processes, you are certified as a skilled professional who *consults* with friends associates and family, in the use of the Holodynamic processes.

The third Circle of Success is for those who want to *facilitate* the shifting of field dynamics. They are trained in the more advanced processes of accessing inherited holodynes, holodynes from parallel dimensions and collective dynamics. Those who graduate from this Circle know how to do all that a Consultant knows how to do and, in addition, becomes skilled at field shifting, reliving and preliving and potentializing systems.

The fourth Circle of Success is designed for those who want to teach Holodynamics so they join with others and practice teaming up to make presentations in classes. When they feel confident they may apply to become a certified *Presenter.*

The fifth Circle of Success is for those who have become competent enough to present entire courses in the Academy without assistance from others. These are the Teachers. This part of the training insures teachers a comprehensive set of tools and skills for instructing others.

The sixth Circle of Success is for those who have mastered teaching the various classes and want to create special projects, accept opportunities to expand the program and teach others to teach. These people can be certified as Masters of Holodynamics. Such people have mastered the entire sequence, including situational and systems dynamics, and become a guide to others in manifesting the future in the present.

The Seventh Circle of Success is for those who qualify at the Doctorial level. They have demonstrated their ability to do all that Masters can do and, in addition, they have written a dissertation and completed an expanded curriculum, including major projects, that are offered by the Academy.

These Seven Circles of Success reflect **seven natural levels of certification.** In addition, each Circle is designed to meet the international accreditation standards of the Academy. Certain hours of classroom instruction, levels of academic competence, field experience and skill competence must be demonstrated and records reviewed before certification is awarded. Each Manual takes you through each step of the way. The summary chart below gives you a brief outline of what is required for certification at each level.

1. ADVOCATE

You qualify as an Advocate when you make the Advocate commitment. You must have successfully completed at least one Unfolding Potential Seminar (Phase I = 20 hours) sponsored by the Academy. You must team up with a certified Advocate who comes to know your work and who will be willing to sponsor you as an Advocate. In all situations, you become an Advocate of Holodynamics when you are using the processes and applying the principles in your daily life.

The Academy also recommends that you do two more things: take more training and keep a personal record of your Advocate activities. You may also arrange to earn a referral fee for those you introduce or recruit into the introductory class.

2. CONSULTANT

In order to be certified as a Consultant, you must continue your training. As a Consultant, you remain an Advocate, assist in two more Phase I classes (40 hours) and in one Phase II Seminar (40 hours). You must also attend a Phase III certification class (30 hours) and demonstrate your ability as a Consultant. The key to serving as a consultant is your ability to apply Holodynamic processes with your friends, family and associates and to consult with those who are attending the follow-up or potentializing groups after the seminars.

This means you demonstrate your ability to guide people as they track their holodynes. You help them cluster and hold the field, and *be there* for the people in the classes. You will be expected to understand the theory and academic background behind these processes. This means completing the recommended readings (at least 30 hours) and an additional 20 hours of related activities. A certified Consultant (who has been your supervisor) must sponsor you as an applicant in order for you to apply to be certified as a Consultant. Once certified, you can charge a professional fee for your services.

3. FACILITATOR

To become a certified Facilitator means you have completed two more Phase I courses as an Advocate (40 hours), helped facilitate a Phase II small group at least once as a Consultant (40 hours) and attended Phase III at least one time (30 hours). It is also recommended, but not required, that you completed one course on Intimacy (30 hours) or its equivalent, and a Phase IV on dynamic systems (40 hours). You will also complete at least 40 more hours of related activities, and additional 50 hours of academic study and reading. You will demonstrate your ability as an Advocate and a Consultant in your life, and also facilitate processes that shift field dynamics at a deep level. You must have a certified Facilitator sponsor you in order to become a Facilitator and, once certified, you may charge a professional fee for your services.

4.   PRESENTER

To become certified as a Presenter, you must have plans to team up with others in teaching a Phase I. In preparation, you should attend two more Phase I courses (40 hours) with this intention in mind and one more Phase II (40 hours). You must attend another Phase III (30 hours) and demonstrate your team teaching ability. You should also attend one additional Phase IV (40 hours), Intimacy (30 hours) and participated in at least one Intensive (80 hours). You will have completed 60 additional hours of extra activities, finished at least an additional 90 hours of in-depth study on the theoretical and historical aspects of what is being taught. You must work with a certified Teacher, who has observed or co-presented with you and is now willing to sponsor you for certification. You will have also documented, according to the Certification Requirements Summary, an outline of the books, articles, and other materials that you have read and understood. You have up-to-date records of your tracking and relive/prelive sessions, and you have demonstrated your knowledge of the code of ethics and professional conduct standards along with a subject mastery list.

5.   TEACHER

To certify as a Teacher, you must complete five of the six segments of the manual series. You have successfully served as Presenter for at least two more Phase I courses (40 hours), a Phase II (40 hours), and at two more intensives (160 hours minimum). You may also get credit for a minimum of three more Phase III courses (90 hours). You must also have served as Presenter in a Phase IV (40 hours), enrolled in a Coaching Program on Manifesting and attended a Business Course in Holodynamics (20 hours). You may attend and Co-Present at additional Intimacy courses for credit (30 hours each). You meet the minimum additional academic standards for professional teachers, which include an additional 100 hours of supervised Holodynamic activities. In addition, you must complete the final exam, submitted your personal portfolio and have a certified Teacher who is willing to sponsor you as a Teacher. You must have achieved the state of being a Holodynamic Teacher.

6.   MASTER

The title *Master* is awarded to those applicants who have completed an approved project, as well as an additional 1000 hours of supervised teaching of Phase I and II, co-presented at Phase III in at least five sessions and be sponsored by a Certified Master. Certification applications are reviewed and approved by the Master's Council prior to issuance of the certificate. All Master Certificates are personally presented by the Director of the International Academy of Holodynamics or his representative.

The official archive for the recording of all certificates is housed within the International Academy of Holodynamics, where all course schedules worldwide are registered and all official materials are published and distributed.

In reading this table, please note that the courses are cumulative. That is, in order to be an Advocate, you must take only one Phase I. As you attend more courses and complete more activities, you will acquire credit toward becoming a Consultant. In order to be certified as a Consultant you must take a total of three Phase I courses (which is two more), one Phase II and a Phase III course. To be a Facilitator requires an additional two Phase I courses (making a total of 5), and so forth. Hours are also cumulative and, thus, by the time you qualify as a Master, you have met the requirements of the International Academy of Holodynamics, which are aligned with world academic standards.

STEPS TO TAKE	I	II	III	IV	INT.	C	BUS	I	OTHER	HOURS OF TRAINING	TOTAL
1. TO BE AN ADVOCATE	1	1							20	100	100
2. TO BE A CONSULTANT	3	2	1						20	200	300
3. TO BE A FACILITATOR	5	3	2	1				1	40	290	590
4. TO BE A PRESENTER	7	4	3	2	1*			2	60	410	1000
5. TO BE A TEACHER	9	5	6	3	3	1	1	+	100	730	1730
6. TO BE A MASTER	+	+	+	+	+	+	+	+	1000	2000	3730

* *Phase I, II and III* refer to the Unfolding Potential series where Tracking, Shifting Fields and Teaching Training is sponsored by the Academy. *Phase IV* refers to the advanced Psychodrama training. *INT* refers to the Intensive combined Phase I, II and III courses. *C* refers to Coaching, *BUS* refers to Business Courses, and *I* refers to Intimacy classes. The column marked *OTHER* refers to supervised activities directly related to the level of certification, *HOURS OF TRAINING* means the cumulative total. All other activities may be logged but no column is provided.

APPENDIX B

ADVOCATE PERSONAL PORFOLIO

This is your official record of your academic and field work as an Advocate. You must always keep your original in a safe place for your own records. A copy of this portfolio will be submitted to the International Academy of Holodynamics' Central Office and to your Sponsor prior to receiving your Certificate as an Consultant.

LOG OF ADVOCATE ACTIVITIES

1. Courses Attended:

I have attended the following courses in Holodynamics:

Course	Location of Course	Presenter	Date	Sponsor Signature
Phase I				
Phase II				
Phase III				
Others (Name)				

My Name: _____

2. Activities:

Identify the Activity	Name the person(s)	Date	Time spent	Sponsor Signature

3. Other Activities:

_____

_____

_____

_____

_____

_____

_____

_____

_____

_____

_____

Activities refer to field experiences directly related to Holodynamic Advocate training or duties such as participating in Holodynamic Courses or meetings, using processes learned in Holodynamic Courses to aid others, taking initiative on approved projects and leadership roles.

REFERAL RECORD

As an Advocate, you may be awarded a referral credit for each person you recruit into a Phase I class. In order for you to obtain the credit, **the person referred must declare on their Registration Intake Form that you referred them to the class**. If more than one Advocate was involved in the process, who gets referral credit must be worked out between the Advocates and reported to the Coordinator. Preferably, this is done without involving the person referred.

Referral credit may be collected as a *cash* reimbursement, if your account is paid in full, or it can be put on your account as *credit* toward Holodynamic classes you are taking or may wish to take in the future. In the true spirit of Holodynamics, this referral credit award is kept confidential. Credit is based upon a percent of the actual amount of money paid, and you, as an Advocate, must follow through to insure the greatest unfolding of potential for each person you refer. Here is a suggested format for keeping track of referrals you have brought into the program.

Name of person referred	Address	Phone	Email	Date	Course

In this conscious universe, we keep what we share. Information is empowered when we align our actions with our intentions. Life energy expands outward from one event horizon to the next as updraft dynamics. When we choose not to align action with intention, the field implodes inward and becomes downdraft. So standing as an Advocate ignites the field and draws through us an alignment of information and energy, an "inner intensity" or "clear intention" that lifts everyone around us. Like a tide on the ocean of consciousness, we are lifted toward fulfilling more of our potential. Sharing this state of being creates a collective coherence that further supports the unfolding of our potential. What we share resides forever in us.

A TOPOLOGICAL MIND MODEL
By V. Vernon Woolf Ph.D.

The combination of topology, holographics, quantum mechanics and fluid dynamics, with cognitive development and systems analysis allows a new, more comprehensive view of the mind. In this model, the mind is given the shape of a cube and the various functions of the mind are "mapped" topologically as follows:

Figure I - FAMILY BELIEF SYSTEM

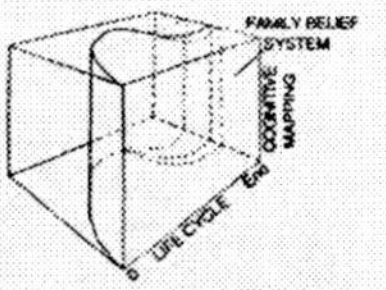

The shaded area represents the holodynamic arena in which all family beliefs, myths, taboos, ethics, and patterns are cognitively "mapped" during a person's life cycle.

Figure II - SOCIOCULTURAL BELIEFS

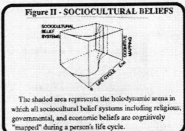

The shaded area represents the holodynamic arena in which all sociocultural belief systems including religious, governmental, and economic beliefs are cognitively "mapped" during a person's life cycle.

Fig. III - THE SIX STAGES OF MATURATION

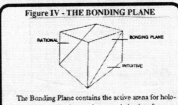

Six sequential stages of maturation show the physical, self-awareness, intimacy, systems, principled, and universal development of the mind. Each stage is fluid, dynamic, and reflects a universal, implicate order of growth.

Figure IV - THE BONDING PLANE

The Bonding Plane contains the active arena for holodynes and acts as an integrative, correlative interface between the linear, particle-focused, rational hemisphere and the holistic wave-focused, intuitive hemisphere.

Figure V - THE INTEREST WAVE

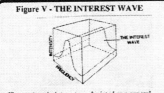

Fluctuations in interest are depicted as a general "quantum" wave function which is controlled by specific holodynes on the bonding plane and sets up a morphogenetic field that controls behavior.

Figure VI - THE MIND MODEL

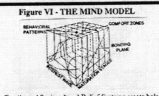

Family and Sociocultural Belief Systems create holodynes that function as subtle attractors, at various stages of growth in the holodynamic arena between the rational and intuitive hemispheres, and produce behavior.

REFERENCES

Section One: Current Books, Articles, email and Web Sites

Holodynamics: www.Holodynamics.com outlines the basic tenants of a Holodynamic view of life and brings up-to-date information worldwide about what is happening in the Holodynamic Society, calendar of courses, materials, articles and much more.

Microtubules: www.hameroff.com The University of Arizona offers extensive courses on consciousness and the vital role played by the microtubules in the biology and psychology of humankind.

Beksey Von, G. *Sensory Inhibition,* Princeton University Press, Princeton.

Bohm, David. *Wholeness and the Implicate Order,* London, Routledge & Kagen 1980

Bracewell, R. N. *The Fourier Transform and its Application,* McGraw-Hill, New York

Brown, W. *Laws of Form,* 1964

Chalmers, D. *The Puzzle of Conscious Experience,* Scientific American, Dec. 1995

Chew, G. S. *The Analytic S-Matrix. A Basis for Nuclear Democracy,* Benjamin, New York

Daugman, F. G. *Uncertainty Relation for Resolution in Space, Spatial Frequency, and Orientation Optimized by Two Dimensional Visual Cortical Filters,* Journal of the Optical Society of America, 2(7), pp. 1160-1169, 1985

Freeman, W. *Correlation of Electrical Activity of Prepyriform Cortex and Behavior in a Cat,* Journal of Neurophysiology, 23, pp. 111-131.

Frohlech, H. *Long-range Coherence and Energy Storage in Biological Systems,* Journal of Quantum Chemistry, II, pp. 641-649, 1968

Gabor, D., *Theory of Communication,* Institute of Eclectically Engineers, 93, pp. 429-441, 1946

Hameroff, S. R. *Information in Processing in Microtubules,* J. Theor. Biol. 98 549-61, 1982

Hameroff, S. R. and Penrose, Roger, *Conscious Events as Orchestrated Space-time Selections,* Journal of Consciousness Studies, 3, No. 1, 1996 p. 36-53.

Hiesenburg, W. *Physics and Philosophy,* Allan and Unwin, 1959

Kant, I. in **Wilber, Ken.** *The Eye of Spirit, An Integral Vision for a World Gone Slightly Mad,* Boston and London, Shambhala, 1997

Kohlberg, Lawrence. *Essays on Moral Development,* Vol. I, The Philosophy of Moral Development, San Francisco, Harper and Row, 1981

Penrose, Roger. *Shadows of the Mind,* Oxford University Press 1994

Piaget, J. *The Child's Conception of the World,* New York. Humanities 1951

Pribram, Karl. *Brain and Perception: Holonomy and Structure in Figural Processing,* Lawrence Erlbaum Assoc., New Jersey 1991

Pribram, Karl. *Quantum Information Processing and the Spiritual Nature of Mankind,* Frontier Perspectives, 6, (1), pp. 12-15, 1996

Marcelja, S. *Mathematical Description of the Response of Simple Cortical Cells,* Journal of the Optical Society of America, 70, pp. 1297-1300, 1980.

Sheldrake, Rupert. *Lives of a Cell,* 1988

Brad, A. *Stairway to the Mind,* N.Y. Copernicus, 1995

Wheeler, J. A. *Assessment of Everett's "relative state" formulation of quantum theory,* Rev. Mod. Phys. 29, pp. 463-5, 1957

Wilber, Ken. *The Eye of Spirit, An Integral Vision for a World Gone Slightly Mad,* Boston and London, Shambhala, 1997

Whitehead, A. N. *Process and Reality,* New York, Macmillan 1933

Woolf, Victor Vernon, see below to the section on Also by Victor Vernon Woolf.

Section Two: General Reading List of "Oldies but Goodies"

Abott, A. *Flatland,* Dover Publications, 1992, New York
This story intuitively helps in understanding the existence of higher dimensional space by describing the plight of two dimensional creatures' encounter with a three-dimensional entity.

Bach, Richard. *Illusions, New York: Dell,1997.*
A wholesome way of looking at life.

Bach, Richard. *One,* **New York: William Moffow and Company, Inc., 1988.**
A curious loving fantasy in harmony with science and spirit at once, a startling door ajar on a different path to finding ourselves.

Becker, Robert 0. and Gary Selden. *The Body Electric: Electromagnetism and the Foundation of Life,* New York: William Morrow and Company, Inc. 1985.

Bloom, Flood E., Arlyne Lazerson, and Laura Hofstadter. *Brain, Mind and Behavior,* New York: Freeman, 1985.
A detailed, biochemical, biological coverage of the nervous system, brain/mind functioning, homeostasis, rhythms of the brain, emotions, learning and memory, malfunctioning and future research on the brain. The book is filled with colored diagrams, pictures and quite a comprehensive coverage of basic information about the brain and the mind processes.

Bohm, David and F. David Peat. *Science, Order, and Creativity,* New York: Bantam Books, 1987.
A dramatic look at the creative roots of science and life. An all-time classic.

Bohm David. *Wholeness and the Implicate Order,* Boston: Ark, 1977.
Bohm introduces the notion of the implicate order in which any element contains enfolded within itself the totality of the universe. His concept of totality includes both matter and consciousness.

Bradshaw, John. *The Family,* Deerfield Beach, FL: Health Communications, Inc., 1988
While limited in some of his perspectives, the author gives some excellent insights into the dynamics of family living.

Branden, Nathaniel. *Breaking Free,* New York: Bantam Books, 1977-
The author offers detailed insights into various subjects regarding human behavior.

Branden, Nathaniel. *Honoring the Self,* Los Angeles: J.P. Tarcher, Inc., 1983.

Branden, Nathaniel. *If You Could Hear What I Cannot Say,* Nash Publishing, Inc., 1972

Branden, Nathaniel. *The Disowned Self,* Los Angeles: Nash Publishing, Inc., 1971

Branden, Nathaniel. *The Psychology of Self-esteem,* Los Angeles: Nash Publishing Co., 1969.

Branden, Nathaniel and E. Devers, Branden. *The Romantic Love Question and Answer Book,* Los Angeles: J. P. Tarcher, Inc., 1982

Briggs, Dorothy Corkille. *Celebrate Your Self - Making Life Work For You.* New York: -Doubleday & Company, Inc., 1977.

Briggs, John P. and F. David Peat. *Looking Glass Universe: The Emerging Science of Wholeness,* New York: Simon and Schuster Inc., 1984.

A fascinating view of quantum physics and some of its implications in modern day life.

Buscaglia, Leo. *Living, Loving & Learning.* New York: Ballantine Books, 1982.

An inspirational treasure for all those eager to accept the challenge of life and to profit from the wonder of love.

Campbell, Jeremy. *Grammatical Man,* New York: Simon and Schuster, Inc., 1982.

An updated, quite comprehensive coverage on the theory of information, the brain and how laws of physics and biochemistry function in the mind. This is an easily readable, integrative book, comparing major theories and updating what is known in the scientific realm of brain/mind functioning. Most major treatises are included as references. The main emphasis is to develop an advance theory on communication processes.

Campbell, Susan. *A Couples Journey: Intimacy as a Path to Wholeness.* San Luis Obispo, CA: Impact Publishers, 1980.

Cole-Whittaker, Terry. *What You Think of Me is None of My Business.* LaJolla, CA.: Oak Tree, 1979.

An entertaining, easily readable, principled book that gives excellent coverage on empowering, abundance, overcoming comfort zones, and how everyone can win.

Crutchfield, J.P. et al. "Chaos". *Scientific American,* (December 1986).

This article introduces current system theories on chaos and turbulence. Surprisingly, depending on what state variables the system is viewed, there can be an underlying order to **what is** perceived as chaos.

Davies, P. *Other Worlds.* Simon and Schuster 1980.

In this narrative text for the layman, Davies overviews the various theories of space, super space (hyperspace) and the universe as described by quantum mechanics including a lengthy description of Everett's many-worlds interpretation of quantum mechanics. In Everett's view, an infinite number of universes exist parallel to our own.

Dossey, Larry. *Space, Time & Medicine.* Boulder, CO: Shambhala Publications, Inc., 1982.

Eisler, Riane. *The Chalice & The Blade.* San Francisco: Harper & Row Publishers, Inc., 1987.

Fanning, Patrick. *Visualization for Change.* Oakland, CA. New Harbinger Publications, Inc., 1988.

A step-by-step guide to using your powers of imagination for self-improvement, therapy, healing and pain control.

Ferguson, Marilyn. *The Aquarian Conspiracy: Personal and Social Transformation in the 1980's,* Los Angeles: J. P. Tarcher, Inc., 1980.

Ferrucci, Piero. *What We May Be.* Los Angeles: J. P. Tarcher, Inc., 1982-

Ford, Edward E. *Why Marriage.* Allen, TX: Argus Communications, 1974.

A reality therapy approach to marriage.

Garfield, Charles A. and Hal Z. Bennett. *Peak Performance.* Los Angeles: J. P. Tarcher, Inc., 1984.

Outlines right-brain experiential training for athletes, that has received international acclaim. Uses clustering, mind journeys and relaxation techniques similar to the Unfolding Potential Seminars.

Gawain, Shakti. *Creative Visualization.* New York: Bantam Books, 1982.

Glasser, William. *Stations of the Mind,* New York Harper & Row, Publishing, Inc., 1981.

Uses perceptual psychology. Shows orders of perception. The first four orders are biochemical, the next six orders are similar to the maturation stages used in the Unfolding Potential Seminars. Many insights about mind functioning that are readable and applicable.

Gleick, James. *Chaos: Making a New Science.* New York: Viking Penguin Inc., 1987.
Records the birth of a new science. This new science offers a way of seeing order and pattern where formerly only the random, the erratic, the unpredictable and the chaotic had been observed.

Goldberg, Herb. *The New Male/Female Relationship.* New York: William Morrow and Company, Inc., 1983.

Goldberg, Philip. *The Intuitive Edge: Understanding Intuition and Applying it in Everyday Life.* Los Angeles: J. P. Tarcher, Inc., 1983.

Gordon, Thomas. *Parent Effectiveness Training. The Proven Program for Raising Responsible Children,* Three Rivers Press; 1st rev. pbk. ed edition (October 31, 2000)

Gould, Roger. *Transformations.* New York: Simon and Schuster, 1979.

Green, E and A. Green. *Beyond Biofeedback.* New York: Dell Publishing Co, 1978.
The authors present their experience, observations and results of studying healing, meditation and parapsychology. Chapter 14 presents a well-referenced "field of mind" theory that supports the concept that all minds are part of a greater universal mind which allows Parapsychological potentials for offering behavior, matter and reality.

Green, Robert J. and James L. Framo (ed.). *Family.* New York: International Universities Press, 1981.

Griscom, Chris. *Ecstasy is a New Frequency.* Santa Fe, NM: Bear & Company, 1987.

Haley, Jay. *Uncommon Therapy: The Psychiatric Techniques of Milton H. Erickson. MD* New York: Norton, 1973.
One of the world's great authorities deals with strategic therapy processes at each stage of the family life cycle. Includes the major issues and therapy processes for each of the stages of development for young adults, courtship, marriage, child rearing, emptiness and old age.

Haridas, Chaudhuri. *The Evolution of Integral Consciousness.* Wheaton, I. L.: Theosophical, 1979.
For someone seriously engaged in the exploration of consciousness.

Harman, Willis and Howard Reinhold. *Higher Creativity.* Los Angeles: J. P. Tarcher, Inc., 1994.
Liberating the unconscious for breakthrough insights.

Heinlein, Robert A. *Sixth Column.* New York: Baen Publishing Enterprises, 1949.

Hofstadter, Douglas R. *Godel, Escher, Bach: An Eternal Golden Braid,* New York: -Vintage Books, 1979.
A metaphorical fugue on minds and machines in the spirit of Lewis Carroll.

Houston, Jean. *The Possible Human.* Los Angeles: J. P. Tarcher, Inc., 1982.

Jampolsky, Gerald, Patricia Hopkins and William Thetford. *Good-bye to Guilt: Releasing Fear Through Forgiveness.* Bantam Dell Pub Group / April 1988

Jampolsky, Gerald. *Love is Letting Go of Fear.* Milbrae, CA: Celestial Arts, 1979.

Jampolsky, Gerald. *Teach Only Love.* New York: Bantam Books, 1983
The seven principles of attitudinal healing.

Jourard, Sidney A. *The Transparent Self.* New York: Van Nostrand Reinhold, 1964.

Kaplan, Helen S. *The Evaluation of Sexual Disorders.* New York: Brunner/Mazel, 1983.

Keen, Sam. *The Passionate Life: Stages of Loving.* San Francisco: Harper & Row, 1983.

Kennedy, Eugene. *The Trouble Book.* New York: Thomas More Association,1976.
An easy-reading manual of principles and processes on overcoming various "troubles." Includes ego and interpersonal troubles.

Keutzer, Camun. *The Power of Meaning: From Quantum Mechanics to Synchronicity,* Journal of Humanistic Psychology. Vol. 24. No.1, (Winter, 1984). pp. 80-94.

Keyes, Ken, Jr. *Handbook to Higher Consciousness.* St. Mary, KY. Living Love Center, 1975.
A practical handbook for living in a world of stress. Explains 12 pathways, seven centers of consciousness, and gives exercises for application.

Kramer, Jeannette R. *Family Interfaces: Transgenerational Patterns.* New York: Brunner/Mazel, Inc., 1985.

A comprehensive coverage on family therapy using clustering, Genograms, interfacing problems. Includes personal applications to the therapist and his own family. Also shows how the principles apply to families, groups and the individual. A modern, comprehensive, excellent text.

Lazarus A. *In the Minds Eye: The Power of Imagery for Personal Enrichment.* Riverside, NJ: Behavioral Books.

Leonard, George. *The End of Sex: Erotic Love After the Sexual Revolution.* Los Angeles: J. P. Tarcher, Inc., 1983.

Leonard, George. *The Transformation: A Guide to the Inevitable Change in Humankind.* Los Angeles: J. P. Tarcher, Inc., 1981.

Maclaine, Shirley. *Out on a Limb.* New York: Bantam Books, 1983.
The author describes her consciousness awakening to experience the universal mind.

Macy, Joanna Rogers. *Despair and Personal Power in the Nuclear Age.* Philadelphia: New Society Publishers, 1983.

Mandler, George. *Mind and Body.* New York Norton, 1984.
An updated research review on what is known about the brain, the body, the mind and emotions. Covers the historical, theoretical aspects of consciousness, emotion, autonomic arousal, biology, anxiety, stress and many other aspects. An excellent text.

McWaters, Barry. *Conscious Evolution: Personal and Plane Transformation.* Los Angeles New Age Press, 1991.

Moss, Richard. *That I That is We.* Millbrae, CA. Celestial Arts, 1981.

O'Connell, April and Vincent. *Choice & Change: The Psychology of Adjustment Growth and Creativity.* Englewood Cliffs, NJ: Prentice-Hall, Inc., 1980.

Patent, Arnold M. *You Can Have It ALL.* Piermont, NY: Money Mastery Publishing , 1987.
The art of winning the money game and living a life of joy.

Paul, Jordan and Margaret Paul. *Do I Have To Give Up Me To Be Loved By You?* Minneapolis: Comp Care Publications, 1983.

Pearce, J. C. *Crack in the Cosmic Egg.* Thriftbooks, WA, a Quokka Book, 1984
This well-referenced scientific and philosophical study examines the nature of paradigm shifts through human history. The author supports with numerous references the motion that our objective reality is created by a universal mind in which we all participate. This allows paranormal phenomena

Pearce, J. C. *Exploring the Crack in the Cosmic Egg.* Thriftbooks, WA, a Quokka Book, 1986
Pearce continues his study exposition that "objective reality" is created by our universal minds and how we access this creative potential.

Pearce, J.C. *Magical Child.* New York: E. P. Dutton, 1977.

Pearce discusses the maturing of the mind and the importance of "magical thinking" ie: fantasizing, creative visualization, etc. His model includes such concepts as a "Primal matrix' or universal mind where intelligences, not only communicate beyond space-time but can alter reality by thought.

Peat, F. David. *Synchronicity. The Bridge Between Matter and Mind.* New York: Bantam Books, 1997.

David wrote the introduction to Vern Woolf's book on Holodynamics and, in this book he lays open some of the implications of quantum physics to social relationships.

Peck, M. Brad. *The Different Drum: Community Making and Peace.* New York: Simon and Schuster, 1987.

Peck, M. Brad. *People of the Lie.* New York: Simon and Schuster, 1983.

Peck, M. Brad. *The Road Less Traveled.* New York Simon and Schuster, 1978

A close examination to one's mental health as it relates to pain and risk to produce growth. An easily readable, principled perspective on human dynamics. Excellent insight, great labeling ability.

Peters, Thomas J. and Robert H. Waterman, Jr. *In Search of Excellence.* New York: Warner Books, 198Z

Lessons from America's best-run companies.

Pirsig, Robert M. *Zen and the Art of Motorcycle Maintenance.* Bantam Books, 1994.

An experiential story of a man's journey out of his saboteurs. Excellent reading.

Rose, Colin. *Accelerated Learning.* New York Dell Publishing Co, Inc., 1985.

Rubin, Theodore Isaac. *One to One: Understanding Personal Relationships.* New York: The Viking Press, 1983.

Rubin, Theodore Isaac. *Reconciliations: Inner Peace in an Age of Anxiety.* New York: The Viking Press, 1980.

Rucker, Rudy. *The Fourth Dimension.* Boston: Houghton Mifflin Company, 1984.

A guided tour of the higher universe.

Russell Peter. *The Global Brain.* Los Angeles, J. P. Tarcher, Inc., 1983.

Drawing on such diverse disciplines as biology, sociology, physics, philosophy, mathematics and mysticism, the author takes us on an exploration of humanity's role and potential as it might be seen through the eyes of the planet.

Sack, Oliver. *The Man Who Mistook His Wife for a Hat.* New York: Harper & Row Publishers, Inc., 1985.

Satir, Virginia. *Peoplemaking.* Palo Alto, CA.: Science and Behavior, 1972.

A classic by one of the world's great therapists. Deals with family dynamics, rules, mapping and extension into the larger society. Many examples and helpful processes are included.

Sauber, S. Richard, Luciano L'Abate and Gerald R. Weeks. *Family Therapy.* Rockville, MD: Aspen Systems, 1985.

An excellent dictionary of most therapeutic processes and how they apply to specific circumstances. Gives all the terms and references as to where each term originated in the evolution of advanced therapy.

Saul, Leon J. *The Psychotic Personality.* New York: Von Nostrant Reinhold Company, 1981

Scarf, Maggie. *Intimate Partners,* New York: Random House, Inc., 1987.

The author gives us a definitive book on marriage, how love relationships are formed, and how they change over the course of the marital cycle.

Sheldrake, Rupert. *A New Science of Life.* Los Angeles: J. P. Tarcher, Inc., 1981.

Small, Jacquelyn. *Transformers: The Therapists of the Future.* Marina Del Rey, CA: -DeVorss & Company, Publisher, 1982.

Smothermon, Ron. *Transforming: Number One.* San Francisco: Context, 1980.
This book discusses the states of integrity that transform your life. Insight to help you love yourself and others and understand the roadblocks between your heart and the hearts of others.

Smothermon, Ron. *Winning Through Enlightenment.* San Francisco: Context, 1980.
This book will challenge the part of your mind which denies "what is" in your life. It will challenge the illusions that destroy your aliveness, your attempts to get your life to work by blaming others for the experiences you create and the distortions that keep you stuck in feelings of separateness.

Speck, Ross V. and Carolyn L Attneave. *Family Networks.* New York: Vintage, 1973.
An excellent outline of how interaction dynamics occur to form family and cultural belief systems. Showing how networking processes individually within families and within systems.

Steiner, Claude M. *The Other Side of Power: How to Become Powerful With Being Power Hungry.* New York: The Grove Press, Inc., 1981.

Steiner, Claude M. *Scripts People Live.* New York: The Grove Press, Inc., 1974.

Stone, Hal and Sidra Winkelman. *Embracing Our Selves.* Marina Del Rey, CA: DeVorss & Company, Publisher, 1985.

Schwartz, David L. *The Magic of Thinking Big.* New York: Simon and Schuster, Inc., 1987.

Talbot, Michael. *Beyond the Quantum.* New York: Macmillan Publishing Company, 1986.
An intriguing inquiry into the roller-coaster rise of modern, speculative physics, focusing on the work of Sheldrake, Hoyle, Bohm and Eccles.

Tart, Charles T. (ed.). *Transpersonal Psychologies.* London: Routledge and Kegan Paul, 1975.

Tart, Charles T. (ed.). *Waking Up: Overcoming the Obstacles to Human Potential.* Boston: Shambhala Publications, Inc., 1986.

Thom R. *Structural Stability and Morphogenesis.* Reading, MA: W. A. Benjamin Inc., 1975.
This advanced mathematical text applies topological systems theory and catastrophe theory to describe phenomena in biology, embryology and general self-organization of systems.

Thomas, Lewis. *The Lives of a Cell: Notes of a Biology Watcher.* New York: Bantam Books Inc., 1974.

ViBrad David. *The ViBrad Method: A Revolutionary Program for Understanding Self Understanding.* Boston: Houghton Mifflin Company, 1984.

Waitley, Dennis. *Seeds of Greatness.* Old Tappan, NJ: Revell, 1983.
A motivational book on principles. Includes self-worth, creative energy, responsibility, wisdom, purpose, communication, faith, adaptability, perseverance and a general perspective that is positive. Easily readable and directly applicable.

Walsh, Roger N. and Frances Vaughn. *Beyond Ego: Transpersonal Dimensions in Psychology.* Los Angeles: J. P. Tarcher, Inc., 1980.

Warsha, T. *Rich is Better.* New York: Doubleday & Company, Inc.
How women can bridge the gap between wanting and having it all: financially, emotionally and professionally. Includes charts, graphs, exercises and negotiating scripts.

Watzalwick, P. *The Situation is Hopeless But Not Serious.* Riverside, NJ: Behavioral Books.
How individuals manage to turn themselves into their own worst enemies.

Weiss, Brian L. *Many Lives, Many Masters.* New York: Simon and Schuster, Inc., 1988
A classic in self-discovery and parallel world influences.

Westwood, John (ed.). *Awakening the Heart.* New York: Shambhala Publications Inc., 1983.

Wilber, Ken. *The Atman Project.* Wheaton, IL: Quest, 1980.
This book is philosophically integrative, comprehensive and profound; a classic for scholars. It is developmental in its theory presentation. Covers ego development, causal potency, consciousness and unconsciousness, as well as a sequential development of the mind.

Wilber, Ken (ed.). *The Holographic Paradigm and Other Paradoxes.* Boston: Shambhala Publications, Inc., 1982.
Explores the leading edge of science and the Holodynamic universe.

Wilber, Ken. *Odyssey: A Personal Inquiry into Humanistic and Transpersonal Psychology.* Journal of Humanistic Psychology. Vol. 22. No.1 (Winter 1982), pp. 57-90.

Wilber Ken (ed.). *Quantum Questions.* Boston: Shambhala Publications, Inc., 1984.
Mystical writings of the world's great physicists.

Williams, Robert H. and John Stockmyer. *Unleashing the Right Side of the Brain.* Lexington, MA: Stephen Greene Press, Inc., 1997.
A systematic approach for unlocking creative potential.

Wolf, Fred Alan. *Parallel Universes.* New York: Simon and Schuster, 1989.

Wolf, Fred Alan. *Star Wave.* New York: Macmillan Publishing Company, 1984.
The concepts of quantum physics are applied to the study of human consciousness and the human mind.

Wolff, F. M. Pathways Through Space. New York: Warner Books, 1973.
Merrill-Wolff has developed the ability to enter a state of infinitely expanded consciousness. The author gives a practical guide to reaching spaces of higher consciousness.

Wolff, F. M. *The Philosophy of Consciousness Without an Object.* New York: Julian Press Inc., 1973.
The author presents a detailed study of his transcendental shift into the universal mind. He wishes to prove that this experience is possible for those who want it.

Woodrew, Greta. *Memories of Tomorrow.* New York: Doubleday & Company, Inc., 1988
One woman's cosmic connection.

Ywahoo, Dhyani. *Voices of Our Ancestors.* Boston: Shambhala Publications, Inc., 1987.

Zdenek, Marilee. *The Right-Brain Experience.* New York: McGraw-Hill Book Company, 1983.
Contains many cases of famous people who have gained success through using their integrative right-brain processes. Also contains many personal experiential exercises, which will enhance your own ability to use your total mind capacities.

Zukav, Gary. *The Dancing Wu Li Masters.* New York: William Morrow and Company, -Inc., 1979.

Zukav, Gary. *The Seat of the Soul.* New York: Simon and Schuster, Inc., 1989.

Section Three: Business

Wheatly, Margaret J. *Leadership and the New Science: Learning about Organization from an Orderly Universe,* Barrett-Koehler Pub., 1992

Chappell, Tom. *The Soul of a Business: Managing for Profit and the Common Good,* Bantam Books, 1993.

Helgesen, Sally. *The Female Advantage - Women's Ways of Leadership,* Doubleday 1990

Connors, Roger. et al. *The Oz Principle - Getting Results Through Individual and Organizational Accountability,* Penguin Books, 2004.

Toffler, Alvin. *The Third Wave,* Bantam Books, New York, 1980.

Section Four: Healing

Chopra, Deepak. *Ageless Body, Timeless Mind - The Quantum Alternative to Growing Old,* Cygnus Books, 2004

Hammerschlag, Carl A. *The Theft of the Spirit - A Journey to Spiritual Healing with Native Americans,* RGA Pub. New York, 1992.

Woolf, Victor Vernon. *The Wellness Manifesto: 95 Treatises on Holodynamic Wellness,* The Int. Academy of Holodynamics, 2005

Section Five: Psychology

Wilber, Ken. *The Spectrum of Consciousness.* Quest Books, 1993.

Redfield, James. *Celestine Prophecy,* Warner Books, New York, 1993

Anderson, Sherry Ruth and Patricia Hopkins. *The Feminine Face of God: the Unfolding of The Sacred In Women,* Cygnus Books, 1991.

Norbu, Namkhai. *The Perfected State,* Snow Lion Books, 1999.

Field, Reshad. *The Invisible Way: A Time to Love, A Time to Die,* Elemental Books, 1979.

Section Six: Also by Victor Vernon Woolf

Woolf, Victor Vernon. *Holodynamics: How to Develop and Manage Your Personal Power,* 1990.
The original 1990 text outlining the basic principles of Holodynamics.

Woolf, Victor Vernon. *The Dance of Life: Transform your world NOW! Create Wellness, Resolve Conflicts and Align your "Being" with nature.* 2005.
The multiple dimensions of reality and how this information applies to those who would like to make a difference in the world.

Woolf, Victor Vernon. *The Holodynamic State of Being: The Advocate's Manual,* 2004-2005.
Manual I in the Circles of Success program sponsored by the International Academy of Holodynamics. Advocates a course in life that unfolds one's fullest potential for the individual and for the planet.

Woolf, Victor Vernon. *Presence in a Conscious Universe: The Consultant's Manual,* 2004-2005.
Manual II in the Circles of Success program sponsored by the International Academy of Holodynamics. Presents training in the first five processes of Holodynamics including transforming holodynes.

Woolf, Victor Vernon. *Field Shifting: The Holodynamics of Integration: The Facilitator's Manual,* 2004-2005.
Manual III for Facilitators in the Circles of Success program sponsored by the International Academy of Holodynamics. Prepares students for certification in the relive and prelive processes.

Woolf, Victor Vernon. *Leadership and Teambuilding: The Holodynamics of Building a New World: The*

Presenter's Manual, 2004-2005.

Manual IV: The use of a Holodynamic approach within systems such as in business and education. Designed for those who wish to be certified as a Presenter in Holodynamic courses.

Woolf, Victor Vernon. *Principle-Driven Transformation: The Holodynamics of the Dance of Life: The Teacher's Manual,* 2004-2005.

Manual V: Principles, processes and stories that prepare those who wish to certify as Teachers in the courses of the International Academy of Holodynamics.

Woolf, Victor Vernon. *The Wellness Manifesto: 95 Treatises on Holodynamic Health,* 2003-2005.

New findings of science that apply to the health industry.

Woolf, Victor Vernon. *The Therapy Manifesto: 95 Treatises of Holodynamic Therapy,* 2003-2005.

New findings of science that apply to the practice of psychotherapy and family therapy.

THE INTERNATIONAL
ACADEMY OF
HOLODYNAMICS

Circles of Success

This is the official **Advocate's Manual** for the first circle in the *Circles of Success* program sponsored by the International Academy of Holodynamics. This manual is part of a series and it is preceded by two texts: (1) *Holodynamics: How to Develop and Mange your Personal Power*, and (2) *The Dance of Life: Transform your world NOW! Resolve conflicts, create wellness and align your "Being" with Nature.*

These texts and the *Circles of Success* courses are designed to help people apply the principles and processes of Holodynamics in their lives and to teach others to do the same. In order to assure the public that each graduate is professionally qualified, a **certification program** has been established. Graduates receive a certificate as they graduate from each *Circle* as follows:

Circle I: the Advocate: Anyone who advocates an inclusive view of reality qualifies at this level. The text for this level is an introduction to *the Holodynamic State of Being* which, once understood, is easy to support. Anyone can be an Advocate.

Circle II: the Consultant: This circle is for those who desire training in *Tracking* and other basic processes of potentialization. Once trained and certified, graduates can then professionally consult with others and are able to charge a fee for services.

Circle III: the Facilitator: The text for this level is *Field Shifting: the Holodynamics of Integration* and is focused on shifting collective information fields through, for example, the *relive* and *prelive* processes. Those who graduate as Facilitators can charge for their work with individuals and within small groups.

Circle IV: the Presenter: When you are ready to teach larger groups you can team up and teach the introductory courses on Holodynamic principles and processes. The text for the course is: *Leadership and Teambuilding: the Holodynamics of Building a New World.* Those who graduate are qualified to team-teach.

Circle V: the Teacher: This course is for those who want to teach without the assistance of others. Their text is *Principle-Driven Transformation: the Holodynamics of the Dance of Life.* Graduates are certified at the Bachelorate level by the Academy and are qualified to teach anywhere in the world.

Circle VI: the Masters Degree: At this level you will write a thesis and initiate a specific field project that makes a difference in the world. You will be certified to teach others to teach.

Circle VII: the Doctorate Degree: Those who successfully graduate at this level will have completed their academic training, written a dissertation and completed a major project in potentialization.

Those who successfully graduate from any *Circles of Success* course will receive a Certificate of Graduation from the Academy. Those who master the courses and complete their Master's training will receive a Master Certificate. The same is true of the Doctorate level.

If you are interested in taking the courses offered by the Academy, contact us at www.holodynamics.com or by email at vernonwoolf@holodynamics.com.

Printed in the United States
109998LV00002B/77-124/A